Northwest Farms INC.
P. O. BOX 3003 • PORTLAND, OREGON 97208
SINCE 1958

LIVING WORLD BOOKS

John K. Terres, Editor

The World of the
Wild Turkey

James C. Lewis

Illustrated with Photographs

J. B. Lippincott Company

Philadelphia and New York

U.S. Library of Congress Cataloging in Publication Data

Lewis, James C   birth date
    The world of the wild turkey.

    (Living world books)
    Bibliography: p.
    1.   Wild turkeys.   I.   Title.
QL696.G2L48   598.6′1   72–2923
ISBN–0–397–00788–4
ISBN–0–397–00912–7 (lib. bdg.)

Frontispiece: Courtesy U.S. Fish and Wildlife Service
All photographs not otherwise attributed are by the author.

To Mom and Dad
Yours and mine

Contents

Foreword

OUR DEPTH OF knowledge about turkeys exists only because many naturalists and wildlife biologists have spent millions of hours studying this fine bird. Over the past fifteen years I have had an opportunity to meet and enjoy the companionship of many of these people. Others from earlier decades I know only as names on their reports, but as my wife will attest I remember their names better than those of my next-door neighbors. This book, then, is based on the work of many men.

Some will shudder at my anthropomorphic phrases. I do not consider myself a vitalist or a mechanist. But I do believe we are fooling ourselves when we credit man alone with the ability to have emotions or think abstractly, and I have chosen to impute to turkeys, for whom I have great respect, some humanlike feelings.

As I complete this work, I think with gratitude of the many people who contributed to my appreciation for nature and guided my training. Besides my parents I wish to thank Dr. Warren W. Chase, Charles E. Friley, Jr., Dr. George A. Petrides, Roy Anderson, Sumner A. Dow, Dr. John A. Morrison, and H. L. Holbrook. My wife, Marian, my children, and John K. Terres helped make this book a reality.

Meet the Wild Turkey

MORNING DEW still glistened on the grass as we waited in our blind near the forest edge. Hidden from the sight of a bird or any other animal, we saw a light breeze shake the oak leaves and bluegrass outside our blind. Small white clouds drifted across the sky. The silence was broken by the plaintive cry of a wood pewee, then the loud flickerlike call of a pileated woodpecker deep in the forest.

Suddenly we heard a faint sound from somewhere among the trees just beyond the woods border. Watching sharply we saw a slight movement near the forest floor. Had that odd-shaped stump been there before, unseen against the black and gray of early morning? Seconds passed—a minute—then two. We began to see a more distinctive shape in the shadows. Then, with cautious but graceful steps, a wild turkey, the king of America's forest birds, walked into the sunlight at the clearing's edge.

The gobbler paused, then stretched his neck and turned his head from side to side to view our blind better. We sat silent and motionless. The blind was well constructed and he did not sense our presence. The turkey relaxed, then leaned forward to pick a few blades of grass.

We saw the 9-inch beard that hung from his chest like a black graduation tassel and iridescent colors of bronze, purple, and red reflected from his breast. He was only a hundred feet away. Through our binoc-

13

ulars we could see the red-gray of his legs and his ebony spurs. The flesh gray of his head blended into the blacks and dark browns of his feathered neck, chest, and back, and his tail was a deep chestnut brown.

Then two hens came out to the wood's edge, smaller, trimmer, and drabber but walking with demure grace. The big gobbler showed no sign of recognition at first. Suddenly he ran a few short, quick steps, then turned to partly face the hens. Swinging his wings downward and forward until they touched the ground, he uttered an explosive *vrrromp!* Now, as he moved ahead, his tautly stretched wing feathers vibrated against the ground with a scraping, rustling noise. All his body feathers were puffed out, making him look much larger; his tail feathers were fanned to a full 180 degrees. We saw his fleshy head caruncles become bright red as they filled with the blood of his emotions. With this mating display before the hens, he swung his stiffened neck and head forward and uttered a loud gobble that carried far through the woods.

Though I have seen it a hundred times, I still find this to be one of

The gobbler struts before his hens (Idaho Fish and Game).

Meleagris gallopavo *gobbler, every feather in place* (Lovett Williams).

Adult wild turkey hen (Lovett Williams).

of the head is flat and narrow with very little forehead. The gobbler has several head adornments which distinguish him from the hen: the wattling (fleshy growths hanging from the throat or chin), the caruncles (fatty growths on the side and back of the neck and lower throat), and the leader, frontal caruncle, or snood (the fleshy lobe hanging from above the bill). All of these fleshy parts contain sinus-like tissue with elastic walls and vacant spaces that can fill with blood when the bird is excited.

The head adornments of the gobbler: wattling and caruncles (Oklahoma Department of Wildlife Conservation).

Meet the Wild Turkey

These growths of skin give the male some of his masculine finery, and they are red, white, or blue, depending on the bird's emotional state and the season. The naked areas of the head and neck are richly pigmented, and chromatophore changes create the various colors, which convey a message in much the same way as a deer's tail signals danger or indecision. When the gobbler is in full strut, his wattling and caruncles are bright red and accentuate a whitish skullcap. They become pale blue when the turkey is frightened and blood leaves the sinuses. The head is also red when he threatens another male. The red is from astoxanthin and other carotenoid pigments; the blue from the deeper layer of melanin, according to Hale and Schein.

The yearling wild gobbler lacks the well-developed head adornments and bright coloration of the adult gobbler and still has short plumage on the head. (In contrast, the head adornments of domestic turkeys are larger and are well developed when they are still yearlings.)

The fleshy skin growths of the head are poorly developed in the wild

In full strut the wattling and caruncles become bright red (Ted Borg, South Carolina Wildlife Resources Department).

The hen has small feathers on the head.

The lighter tips of
the breast feathers help to
identify the female.

TOM   HEN

hen, and the head parts are covered with a fine dark plumage. These head and plumage differences between male and female turkeys are dependent sex characteristics in hens. Males that are castrated continue to grow the normal male plumage, but when a hen's ovaries are removed, she develops the plumage of a male. The reason is that the functioning ovaries produce a hormone which suppresses the male characteristics in hens.

The body feathers of a typical wild hen have light brown, buff, or white tips (the color depending on the subspecies). As a result her body has a much lighter appearance than that of the gobbler, whose body feathers are black-tipped.

Feathers of turkeys are like those of other birds. There are three

The rump feathers of
the western subspecies are
whiter.

types—vaned, down, and filoplume. The vaned (also called contour) feathers cover most of the body and give the turkey its streamlined appearance. The short, fluffy down feathers, especially noticeable in young poults (as the chicks are called), are closer to the turkey's body, beneath the contour feathers. Their chief function is to conserve heat. The filoplumes or "bristles" are those small feathers on the male's head and on the frontal caruncle (Schorger, 1966).

At hatching, the poult's down is light yellowish brown. At six weeks of age the general body color is a light chocolate brown. By the twentieth week the darker brown, adultlike plumage of the breast and upper back reflects shades of iridescent bronze, green, brown, blue, red, and purple. The iridescence is due to feather structure. In iridescent feathers, the ends of the barbules that fringe the barbs of the feather are broadly flattened and twisted 90 degrees, with the flat surface uppermost. This surface is covered with thin laminated layers of horn which act like raindrops or tiny prisms to produce the rainbow colors. When sunlight strikes the turkey's feathers, the light, refracted at a certain angle, is separated into the beautiful colors we see as the bird moves about.

The tail coverts (rump feathers) of Eastern and Florida turkeys are brown with an iridescent bronze or copper sheen and with tips of brown or buff. In the Merriam's, Mexican, and Gould's turkeys these upper tail feathers are whitish. The rectrices (long tail feathers) are brown mottled with black; they are tipped with a lighter brown or white, depending on the subspecies to which the turkey belongs. In the eastern races the tips are chestnut or light chocolate brown. The western subspecies, the Rio Grande, Merriam's, and Mexican turkeys, have whiter tips to the tail feathers.

Since the domestic bronze turkey was developed from the Mexican subspecies, it also has white-tipped tail feathers. In Eastern, Florida, and Rio Grande turkeys the rectrices are a single color except near the tip. In the Merriam's turkey they are barred with black and cinnamon and the rump tends to be black. In the Mexican turkey the rectrices are vermiculated or mottled, and the rump is distinctly marked or barred by green iridescence.

Odd colorations occasionally occur in turkeys just as in other wild animals. Albino and partly albino turkeys have been reported in Virginia, West Virginia (Bailey, 1955a), Texas (Thomas, *et al.,* 1964a), Florida, and Montana (Jonas, 1964). Other forms of abnormal coloration are a red (erythristic) gobbler and a red and white gobbler in Florida (Williams, 1964); black or melanistic turkeys reported by Mosby and Handley; and a combination of erythrism, melanism, and albinism in turkeys from southern Georgia. Lovett Williams (1964) and Robert Jonas (1966) have also observed turkeys without the normal barring on the long primary feathers of the wings.

The so-called beard of the wild turkey is a secondary sex character of males. Its texture is almost like that of a horse's tail, and it sprouts from the middle of the breast like a misplaced shaving brush. In

The beard is made up of another type of feathers.

The beard of the yearling gobbler is barely visible during his first spring (Texas Parks and Wildlife Department).

reality it is just another bunch of feathers. Feathers arise from follicles, or small glands in the skin. A. W. Schorger (1957) found that the bristles of the beard share characteristics of both filoplume and contour feathers; he called them mesofiloplumes. From one to fourteen mesofiloplumes arise from a single follicle. The bundles have the appearance of branching because the bristles stick to one another by a scalelike cementing material.

The length of the beard and the number of bristles in it do not relate to the turkey's age except in a general way. Schorger examined beards containing as many as 677 bristles; the longest he measured was 325 millimeters (about 13 inches). The bristles continue to grow throughout the turkey's life, but wear and breakage, as it brushes against undergrowth and drags on the ground, limits beard length.

Bearded hens tend to have some of the male head adornments.

The young-of-the-year gobbler has a small beard which begins to jut out from the breast feathers in fall or early winter. By April the same gobbler will have a beard 3 to 4 inches long. The average adult gobbler's beard will extend 8 to 9 inches. The maximum length of a beard is probably slightly more than 13 inches.

The beard is, of course, more characteristic of the gobbler. That its growth is not prevented by castration, however, indicates that it is a sex characteristic not dependent on a male hormone, according to Scott and Payne and Marsden and Martin.

Beards on hens are not rare. Robert D. McDowell examined 577 Eastern hens in Virginia, and 4 were bearded. Eight of 30 mature Merriam's hens had beards, but only 1 of 28 two-year-old hens were bearded. Of 45 Merriam's hens trapped in New Mexico, 29 percent were bearded (D. MacDonald, personal communication). Both age and certain genetic traits may increase the probability that hens will be bearded.

One might suspect a bearded hen to be infertile, but in three areas of southern Texas, where beards were present on 3 to 7 percent of the hens, Samuel Beasom (1970) found no significant difference between the productivity of bearded and unbearded hens.

Hens with beards may be more aggressive; they are often treated with greater respect by other hens. Beasom (1968) made observations on a flock of 35 hens in Texas. There were 2 hens in the group with beards estimated to be 8 and 5 inches long. The hen with the longer beard was dominant over all other hens, and the other bearded hen held the number-two position in the peck order.

Although beards as long as 8 inches have been measured on hens, most are no longer than 3 to 4 inches. Most states with gobblers-only hunting laws consider a bearded hen legal game, because hunters rely heavily on the beard to identify gobblers, especially in the fall.

Multiple beards grow, occasionally, on both gobblers and hens. There are records of both Rio Grande and Eastern turkeys with five distinct beards. A gobbler shot in 1969 in Oklahoma had five beards measuring 10, 9, 5, 3, and ½ inches for a total of 27½ inches of beard.

Another characteristic that distinguishes the sexes is the spur, a stiff horny growth on the back of the turkey's leg a few inches above the foot. The hardness of these growths is indicated by the fact that Indians used them for arrowheads. Where they connect to the leg they are oval-shaped. On adult gobblers, spurs average about 1 inch long and the maximum is about 1¼ inches, tapering and curving upward to a sharp point. They are smooth and have a shiny ebony appearance. In hens and juvenile gobblers they are little more than grayish bumps; however, there are exceptions, and occasionally hens have spurs.

Hunters, bird watchers, and biologists know several turkey characteristics that permit them to distinguish, at a distance, the gobbler from the hen. The gobbler is generally larger, has a lighter-colored head, a darker body, and a beard. The hen is smaller and has a darker head and paler body. The young gobbler is less distinct during the

Spurs of adults help identify the male. The gobbler on the left is younger.

The hen (right) is smaller than the young gobbler (Lovett Williams).

fall before his beard and fleshy head growths are apparent. However, at this season he is usually traveling with hens and can be compared with them. He has sparser feathering on the head and neck and his body appears darker than the hens' because he has black-tipped plumage on his breast and back by the time he is five months old.

The largest game bird of North America, the wild turkey reaches its full growth when two years old. However, the reported weights of Eastern wild turkeys killed by American colonists indicate that earlier ones might have differed in some respects from our present-day birds. Weights of 27 to 35 pounds seem to have been more common at that time. Some were said to weigh as much as 63 pounds (Schorger, 1966), more than today's domestic turkeys weigh after generations of breeding. Unfortunately the Boone and Crockett Club has no category for turkeys. Certainly 27.5 pounds for an Eastern gobbler in Missouri, 25 pounds for a Florida gobbler (Powell, 1965), 28 pounds for a Merriam's turkey from New Mexico, and 22 pounds for a Rio Grande bird must be near-record weights for wild turkeys. J. S. Ligon listed the maximum weight for a male Merriam's turkey as 35 pounds but did not make it clear that he ever weighed a bird that size. Others who weighed many Merriam's turkeys failed to list any larger than the 28-pound bird (Hoffman, 1962; Jonas, 1966; Suetsuga and Menzel; MacDonald, 1961). At any rate, a wild gobbler weighing more than 20 pounds is a trophy bird today in many parts of the East, and one over 25 pounds is a rarity. Among several hundred turkeys I examined, the largest was a 21-pound gobbler in Tennessee weighed in late April.

The original turkeys from the Northeast and from the Lake states may have been slightly larger than other Eastern turkeys, just as white-tailed deer in these areas tend to be bigger than the Southern whitetail. A high percentage of the birds that live year round in the North have larger bodies than their relatives living in warmer climates. A large body is an advantage in a cold climate because of the heat economy created by the more favorable ratio of body surface to volume. The principle that animals of a species are usually larger in northern latitudes than their relatives in southern latitudes is known as Bergmann's rule.

Even these possible size differences, however, would not be enough to explain some of the larger weights of wild turkeys reported by colonists, and probably the great weights reported for some turkeys were estimates. A. W. Schorger (1966:88) quoted a humorous bit of advice of 1881 from a "J. E. R.": "When you kill a gobbler of twenty-five or thirty pounds do not weigh him; they generally resent such a proceeding by falling off from five to ten pounds."

Even now we find considerable variations among the weights of turkeys living in different parts of the United States, owing to the subspecies present in each locale and its history (if any) of crossbreeding with domestic turkeys. In some parts of the United States there has been considerable hybridizing, which began with the first mixing of wild turkeys with tame turkeys around farmsteads. A. Starker Leopold (1944) found that domestic turkey chicks were 27 percent heavier than wild poults of the same age. Hybrids were intermediate in body weight and averaged 3 pounds heavier than pure wild turkeys.

In Missouri, where some hybrid flocks exist, John B. Lewis wrote that adult hens varied from 8 to 13.5 pounds and gobblers from 15 to 27.5 pounds (personal communication). Adult hens averaged only 9.2 pounds in West Virginia (R. W. Bailey, personal communication) as compared to 11.5 in Missouri. Adult gobblers averaged 21 pounds in Missouri and only 16.9 pounds in West Virginia. The Florida wild turkey tended to be smaller, averaging 8.4 pounds for the hen and 14.5 for the adult male. Merriam's turkeys in Nebraska averaged 9.5 pounds for the hen and 17.8 pounds for the gobbler according to Suetsuga and Menzel. The largest wild gobbler examined in Nebraska weighed 26 pounds. Adult Rio Grande gobblers examined by W. Caleb Glazener (personal communication) in Texas ranged from 13 to 22 pounds; hens weighed from 6 to 10 pounds.

Aside from depending on a bird's age, sex, and subspecies, weights also vary with the season and the crop contents of the individual turkey. The crop is the name for the pouchlike enlargement of the lower gullet (throat) in which food is held prior to passing into the gizzard (muscular stomach). The crop sometimes contains as much as 300 to 400 cubic centimeters of food, or more than two-thirds of a pint. When the crop is full, it may weigh a pound or between 5 and 10 percent of the bird's total weight. Thus crop contents can significantly influence a wild turkey's total weight. The volume of foods found in the turkey's crop in southwestern Texas averaged 144 cubic centimeters for January to March, 97 cc. for April to June, 51 cc. for July to September, and 204 cc. for October to January (Korschgen, 1967).

Turkeys are usually heaviest in late winter and early spring if they have not suffered from malnutrition during the winter. In South Dakota, the average weight of both gobblers and hens increased 12 ounces between January and March, according to Petersen and Rich-

The gobbler accumulates fat in preparation for the mating season (Ted Borg, South Carolina Wildlife Resources Department).

ardson. Generally the adults are lightest in late summer, after the physical demands of the mating and brooding season and the molt of the feathers. Food intake is also reduced during hot weather. In autumn, turkeys begin to gain in weight again, as they feed on an abundant supply of acorns, nuts, and pine seeds, known collectively to the biologist as "mast." Weight changes in turkeys correspond with the annual variations found in other wild birds, such as song sparrows, catbirds, mourning doves, cardinals, and bobwhite quail. The normal annual weight fluctuation for wild turkeys may be 15 percent or more of their total live weight. The late winter weight increase in the hen results from the increase of her body fat desposits and the increased size of her reproductive organs in preparation for the mating season. In the gobbler, fat accumulates mainly on the breast, in preparation for the mating season when he eats less. This spongy layer of fat, known as the "breast sponge," acts as an energy reservoir when he is not feeding regularly. The breast sponge is most apparent in a gobbler examined early in the spring, when it may account for 11 percent of his weight. By early summer, much of the fat reservoir has been used up.

As in all birds, the endocrine glands of wild turkeys—pancreas, adrenals, thyroids, ovaries, testes, and pituitary—regulate many body functions and they also determine external characteristics. These glands pour hormones into the bloodstream which are then carried to other organs of the body. The hormones are involved in breeding, body and feather growth, molting, pigmentation, and other physiological functions.

Hormones act on the central nervous system and thereby affect behavior. For example, the hormone prolactin, produced by the pituitary gland, causes broodiness in hens; the male hormone androgen in gobblers is responsible for sexual behavior (gobbling, courtship, copulation) and aggressive behavior toward other gobblers. The gobbler strongly influenced by androgen and male breeding behavior is the turkey most likely to respond to the hunter's turkey caller, which usually imitates the so-called "yelp" of a hen ready for mating.

The endocrine system and the nervous system exercise almost complete control over the functioning of the turkey. The size and presumably the capability of the glands and brain are genetically inherited. A. Starker Leopold (1944), who studied wild, hybrid, and domestic turkeys in Missouri, found differences in the sizes of their glands and brains among the three groups. He demonstrated that wildness and domesticity are inherited, and turkeys endowed with "wildness" follow a behavior pattern that promotes survival of the race and of the individual in the wild. Wild poults hide and freeze in response to the hen's warning cluck, while hybrids scatter; thus the more wary turkeys have a survival advantage. Again, hybrid turkeys breed and nest earlier; therefore their poults may face critical food shortages and unfavorable weather.

Such studies of the nervous and endocrine systems help to explain why wild turkeys survive better than hybrid or domestic turkeys and serve as reasons why sportsmen's groups should not release domestic or hybrid turkeys to increase the populations of their local wild flocks. They also indicate the probable reasons why pen-reared or game-farm turkeys fail to occupy wild habitats in places where wild-trapped turkeys later become established.

The typical life span for a wild turkey has been established by means of studies of birds banded as poults or subadults and recovered in later years. Wild turkeys live longer than many other birds, although the majority die before they are two years old (Powell, 1963; Bailey and Rinell, 1968). James Powell reported a Florida turkey hen that survived at least nine years, one banded eight years, and three banded seven years. Powell's study indicated that the average life expectancy was about eighteen months. Henry Mosby and Charles Handley reported gobblers that were thought to be seven and twelve years of age. In West Virginia, R. Wayne Bailey and Kermit Rinell (1968)

31

indicated that hens four and five years old were not uncommon. One Merriam's gobbler survived at least nine years (Ligon), and Edward A. Walker (personal communication) reported a Rio Grande male that lived almost fourteen years. Banded Rio Grande hens survived nine and six years. Regardless of the subspecies, a turkey five years old can compliment itself on its survival capabilities. Turkeys nine years or older are probably rare.

Spring

A WARM CHINOOK blows across the eastern slopes of the Rockies. Patches of bare ground show wherever the sun's full rays are not blocked by tall ponderosa pines. A flock of Merriam's turkeys moves gracefully through the forest. One bird strides quickly to a patch of ground where the snow has recently melted. With one foot and then the other, it sweeps the accumulated debris backward. The birds are feeding on pine seeds, juniper berries, piñon nuts, snowberry fruit, and an occasional Gambel's oak acorn. They move quietly except for low clucks and yelps. There are twenty-nine hens of different ages. Three yearling gobblers stay near the edge of the flock.

Other gobblers are elsewhere in the forest, segregated in their bachelor flocks. The promise of spring is in the breeze as the air temperature rises. Toms express their uneasiness with resounding gobbles. The amount of androgen pulsing through their bodies has increased as daylight lengthens. As they become more aggressive, each male flock will soon separate into smaller groups of one to three courting gobblers.

The male can be heard sending forth an occasional gobble at any season, but in early spring almost any loud noise between 200 and 6,000 cycles per second may stimulate him to gobble—a sonic boom, the hoot of a barred owl, or a car door slamming. Once, while taking a census of turkeys, I stood at one spot at daybreak and heard five individual males in as many different directions. The gobble of one was answered by another until the hollows resounded with their overlapping calls. In early spring when the birds are still in large flocks, the gobble of one member of a flock provides a stimulus for all others to reply. This type of group stimulus, called social facilitation, can be observed in a number of situations with birds that are gregarious (living in flocks or groups) like turkeys.

The gobbling season is apparently triggered by increasing day length and temperature. When turkeys were experimentally subjected to fourteen hours of artificial light beginning in December (Margolf *et al.*) or to higher temperatures (Burroughs and Kosin), their sexual maturity was advanced several months. Increasing day length is apparently monitored by the turkey's central nervous system through the eyes and skin and the information then transmitted to the pituitary gland. The pituitary gland increases production of hormones which act on the gonads. The gonads then produce hormones to stimulate breeding behavior. Gobbling associated with courting begins in late

Two gobblers in a cypress glade at dawn (Lovett Williams).

Spring

February or March in the South and early April in the North. Most courting activities end by May or mid-June.

The sound of the gobble varies with the individual, but a high-pitched or hoarse gobble is generally from a young gobbler. The older gobbler produces a deep bass sound.

Some consider the gobble a territorial signal or song like that sung by many other birds—the robin, for example. But the gobbler does not defend a fixed area and drive away all other males. The only area he defends is that within a few yards of the hens.

Under ideal conditions the gobbler can be heard a mile away. Strong wind, rough topography, and heavy foliage may reduce this distance to a hundred yards.

One major function of gobbling is to help hens and gobblers find each other, and its intensity seems to depend on the closeness of the hens. Gobbling is most frequent from the time the tom leaves the roost until he meets a hen. The hen generally approaches the tom, and, unless he is already busy with other hens, he will move toward her. After they meet he becomes less vocal. Later in the spring, when the hen starts incubating her clutch and no longer joins the tom, gobbling is more prolonged, sometimes lasting until 10 or 11 A.M.

Of course gobbling attracts animals other than fellow turkeys. Foxes, bobcats, and coyotes have all been known to take advantage of the gobblers' "singing" to invite themselves to dinner. Occasionally their stalk is successful but not often enough to make these predators a problem.

The gobble is more than an expression of sexual need. It fits several emotional situations. At times it appears to be nothing more than a salute to a good day or a feeling of well-being. In other situations it appears to be a threat or an expression of fear.

J. S. Ligon wrote of an experience which suggests the use of gobbling as aggressive behavior or as a threat. A group of Merriam's turkeys were feeding along the edge of a harvested oat field when a

35

golden eagle flew toward them. They ran under some young pines. The eagle ran about on the ground, trying to catch a turkey. "However," Ligon wrote, "a dozen gobblers rallied near by and began a great demonstration, gobbling and fussing in such manner as to cause the eagle to abandon the chase and leave the gobbler assembly in command" (Ligon, page 9).

The gobble is most frequently associated with spring and strutting turkeys. Sometimes the gobbler can be heard about dusk, before or just after he goes to roost. Turkeys may gobble for long periods on moonlit nights; however, the main gobbling period is from a little before daybreak until two or three hours after sunrise.

Strutting and the pulmonic puff sound are usually associated with gobbling during courting behavior. (Old-timers say that the only thing that can be mistaken for a courting turkey is a politician.) The male struts before he gobbles, holding the large wing feathers rearward

When the gobbler struts, the tail feathers fan out into a 180-degree circle and the wing primaries brush against the ground (Tennessee Game and Fish Commission).

and near the ground, spreading the tail feathers to a full fan, raising the body feathers, and pressing the head and neck rearward against the back feathers. Meanwhile the snood is elongated and the head color is red. The gobbler takes three to five short, stiff steps with the wing feathers pressed tautly against the ground. As he moves forward these feathers brush against the soil, grass, and leaves, making a *schhhhhhhh* sound, a noise which he also utters as he expells air loudly. The pulmonic sound is made deep within the throat and cannot be heard more than several hundred feet—a *vrrrrrrrrrrrromp* in a bass tone. Then he gobbles. The entire display sounds like this: *schhhhhhhhhh-vrrrrrrrrrrrromp-gobble-gobble-gobble-gobble.*

The gobble is not always preceded by strutting and the pulmonic puff, and turkeys sometimes strut without gobbling. One beautiful spring day when I was hunting and hadn't heard a turkey for several hours, I sat against a tree, imitated the yelp of a hen turkey a few times, and then dozed in the sun. About fifteen minutes later I heard the pulmonic puff and dragging wings, perhaps six times, each time closer, but never with a gobble. It was a weird sound, giving me the feeling that only part of the bird was approaching.

A last feature associated with gobbling is the coloration of the head growths, described in the first chapter. As they fill with blood and redden, they can be expanded or contracted at will; the frontal caruncle may increase in size from 1 to 6 inches.

The tom selects open areas for his courting displays—field borders, old roads, or mature forest with only moderate amounts of undergrowth. Rio Grande turkeys use traditional courting grounds early in the spring, but later they disperse and continue courting near their nesting areas. Eastern turkeys seem quite mobile during courting. I once watched two gobblers courting three hens. They were moving slowly through the woods in a valley below me. Though the gobblers strutted repeatedly, the hens were feeding and appeared indifferent to the males' antics. One hen finally squatted and a gobbler mounted her

37

back and partly extended wings. He trod her with his feet, with much flapping of his wings; then he copulated. Throughout this performance the other gobbler continued to strut and to move slowly with the other hens in the direction they had been traveling. In the ten to fifteen minutes I watched them, no gobbling took place. On other occasions I have followed noisy courting groups that moved at a rate of from one-half to one mile an hour.

The most thorough study of courting behavior among turkeys was that of C. R. Watts (1968) on Rio Grande turkeys, in which colored plastic markers were attached to their wings so that individual birds could be identified from a distance. Watts found that winter flocks of males were composed of one or more sibling (brother) units. (Some of these were not genetically related but were reared together by one or more hens.) Groups of juvenile males often joined flocks of adult males. In toto the typical winter flocks contained between ten and twenty-five individuals consisting of several sibling groups of several age classes, and these groups seemed to retain their composition

The hen seems to ignore her suitor. Note the worn tips on the gobbler's primary wing feathers (Ted Borg, South Carolina Wildlife Resources Department).

for several years except when a member died.

Watts found there was a peck order among the individuals of each sibling group as well as between the various sibling groups. Peck order is a ranking of "who can pick on whom." The dominant bird (alpha) can peck all the others. The second-ranking bird (beta) can peck at everyone inferior to him but cannot peck at the dominant bird. The lowest-ranking bird (omega) is pecked by everyone else and cannot peck anyone. According to Watts, both toms and hens had their own peck order, and fighting was common while the peck order was being established. Sibling groups fought as teams. The position of a sibling group in the peck order was therefore determined by the number of individuals in the group as well as by their physical size and aggressiveness. As a result, groups containing two- or three-year-old birds were usually dominant. The few toms surviving to age four or older were outnumbered and defeated by the younger groups.

Among teams of gobblers, one individual is dominant (Texas Parks and Wildlife Department).

Gobblers of several ages respond to approaching hens (California Department of Fish and Game).

In south Texas, Watts found, the first signs of winter flock breakup came as early as the last week in January. At that time the male sibling groups began gobbling and strutting on traditional display grounds near the hens' winter roost. At first, the males stayed at a distance, but later in the season most of them roosted with the hens. At the beginning of the courting season the hens were still in their large winter flocks of 20 to 150 birds. At that time they would fly from the roost to the display grounds, where they fed and rested for a few hours before moving off.

Watts found that the dominant male sibling group accompanied the hens to the display area but subordinate male groups traveled separately. Then, while the dominant group of gobblers occupied the center of the display ground with the hens, the subordinate male groups would station themselves around the periphery. Members of a sibling unit strutted only a few yards apart, and fighting among sibling groups was common.

Mating early in the breeding season was the duty of the dominant male in the dominant sibling group. An exception was when two hens, widely separated in the flock, were ready to mate simultaneously. Then, while the first male was mating, the dominant male of the

40

second-ranked sibling group mated with the second hen. The dominant male was seldom interrupted during copulation because other members of his group fought off any intruders. Either before or after the dominant male mated, the other members of his "brotherhood" had mock matings, mounting and treading logs, dried cow manure, or the ground.

On the Welder Wildlife Refuge, where Watts conducted his study, the male flocks contained birds that stayed in the same area in the summer. Many of the hens, however, spent the summer off the refuge. After breeding started, the hens that had their summer range outside the refuge began to return to their nesting areas, and by early March the only hens left on the display grounds were those that would stay all summer. These flocks of hens then began splitting into smaller groups and moving out to nesting areas. They were accompanied by sibling groups of gobblers that mated with them and no longer returned to the display grounds. The male flocks retained their same membership from year to year; however, the sibling groups of hens often did not join the nesting group they had joined the previous season. Whenever one group of hens commenced incubation or were unreceptive, the gobbler group moved on, sometimes driving a subordinate group of gobblers away from another group of hens.

The dominant males did almost all the mating, and only rarely did the peck order change within a sibling group. Therefore, the larger and healthier males do most of the breeding. The social behavior of turkeys assures that the most capable individual will pass his genetic characteristics along to future generations and provides a good example of survival of the fittest by natural selection, a basic premise of Darwin's theory of evolution.

Watts did not see yearling males mating but thought they might mate, in May or June, with hens attempting to renest. At that time the juvenile males were still strutting and the adult males had returned to the flocks of which they were members in the winter. Some toms are

The Eastern turkey courts in small groups (H. L. Holbrook).

sexually mature their first spring; fully developed sperms have been found in their testes and they have successfully bred hens. Generally, however, they do not have a chance to mate because they are at the bottom of the peck order.

The courting behavior of the Eastern and Florida turkeys differs slightly from that of the Rio Grande and Merriam's. Since Eastern and Florida turkeys mate in smaller, more intimate groups, there is much less of the carnival atmosphere provided by larger groups of toms and hens. Also, if they have traditional mating grounds, these

Gobblers often court as a team (H. L. Holbrook).

are less distinct than the Rio Grande turkey's. Frequently a single gobbler courts a half dozen hens, although it is not uncommon to find two or even three Eastern turkey gobblers strutting as a group.

Studies in Missouri and Alabama by Barwick and Speake and by Ellis and Lewis indicated that gobblers that team together are often brood mates and form sibling groups like those found among Rio Grande turkeys. Three male poults captured in the same brood in Alabama gobbled together for the next two mating seasons. Then, after the death of one, the two remaining birds shared a strutting ground during the third spring.

Fighting among gobblers is most prevalent in the spring. M. L. Burget reported that young males are the first to fight. They grab each other by their wattles or cheeks and move in a circle, twisting and pulling. Sometimes they flog each other with their wings. As the mating period approaches, the older gobblers begin fighting. Before the gobbler fights, he faces his opponent with the head held high in the characteristic threat posture. The wings are held slightly away from the body and droop as though the gobbler was ready to strut. The tail feathers are partly fanned and the body feathers are sleeked down against the body. The battling pair give a high-pitched trill just before the action begins (Hale and Schein). The fight may start with the birds jumping at each other, like game cocks, with the feet extended forward. Their weapons are the bill, spurs, wings, and feet. They rush each other, and each attempts to grasp its opponent on the loose skin of the head. The wing butts beat the adversary; the spurs and feet push and gouge. Once the heads are grasped the birds' necks become entwined, and the turkeys have a tugging battle.

Some authors, including John James Audubon, have written that injury during these battles is considerable and can be fatal. However, in recent times there has been very little evidence of serious wounding of combatants. Generally the loser receives no more than a few spur punctures and a skinned head or neck. When one of the combatants

43

feels he has been bested, he either moves away or shows submission by lying on the ground with his neck outstretched (Schorger, 1966), a gesture that appeases the winner.

Although the gobbler operates on short rations during the spring, he eats a little between the bouts to establish peck order or on afternoons when he is free from the pressures of courting. By late spring the fat reserves of the breast sponge are exhausted, and the gobbler needs a period of rest and relaxation.

The hen is more sensible about her spring diet. Her mealtimes remain on schedule except during incubation. Tender leaves of grasses and sedges, which appear with warmer weather, provide favored foods. The remnants of last fall's mast and seed crops, dogwood, hackberry, beech, corn, black gum, pecan, hickory, wild grapes, still provide some of her food. When insects begin to stir after their winter inactivity, their lethargic movements make them easy prey for a quick strike with her bill.

She is also selective about her minerals. Like hen pheasants (Sadler) and other game birds in spring, she eats more snails (Korschgen, 1972) and grit containing calcium than at other seasons. The extra calcium is needed for eggshell production.

The hen is receptive to the gobbler's advances every five days or so. A single mating, however, is sufficient to fertilize the hen's entire clutch, and she can lay fertile eggs up to six weeks after mating is discontinued. Shallow pockets in the wall of the upper oviduct serve for sperm storage and have the proper temperature and biochemistry to ensure sperm survival (Grigg). Each ovum (egg), during its development, passes through the oviduct. At that time the stored sperm are squeezed into contact with it, and the egg is fertilized.

Occasionally domestic turkey eggs have matured without fertilization, a type of development called parthenogenesis. An example would be a virgin hen which laid eggs that completed various stages of development but did not hatch. Sometimes, too, the unfertilized eggs hatch and produce fertile offspring (Olsen and Marsden; Schorger, 1966). True parthenogenesis generally produces only males. Its occurrence among turkeys indicates that they are a primitive bird group low in the scale of evolutionary development.

Nesting begins in late March or April over most of the wild turkey's range. In Florida it begins in February. Patches of snow are still visible when Merriam's hens begin their incubation in the mountains in late April. The main period of hatching is March and April for the Florida turkey and May and June for Eastern, Rio Grande, and Merriam's turkeys. Nesting activities are usually completed within three months after they begin, but some hens hatch broods in late July. In Michigan I once saw a brood only a few days old on the eighth of August.

At first, egg laying is irregular, with the hen often skipping a day (Blakey). Gradually it becomes more regular, and the hen lays one egg about every twenty-five hours until one is laid near sundown. Then she skips a day and begins another cycle, laying an egg early in the morning about thirty-six hours later. As egg laying progresses she spends less and less time with the gobbler. She requires fifteen to eighteen days to complete the average clutch, which contains ten to twelve eggs.

Turkeys are indeterminate layers; that is, they stop laying when a sufficiently large clutch stimulates them to begin incubation. If eggs are removed from the nest as soon as they are laid the hen will continue to lay. The stimulus that stops laying must be the feel of a sufficient number of eggs against the breast or the visual stimuli provided by a certain number of eggs.

Low temperatures prior to incubation can be harmful to turkey eggs (Scott). Before incubation begins, the temperature in the nest is only 1 to 2 degrees warmer than the surrounding air. Arnold Hayden (1961), who studied the effect of low temperatures during laying and incubation, placed turkey eggs in natural locations and found that the majority were not harmed by temperatures as low as 18 degrees above

45

zero Fahrenheit. But if they are exposed to prolonged cold weather prior to incubation, the eggs may fail to hatch.

Most hens nest alone but some have been reported nesting together (Schorger, 1966). These groups did not maintain so-called "dump" nests like those in which one duck incubates the eggs laid by several others. The turkey hens nested next to each other, but each incubated her own eggs.

Wild turkeys nest in many places. I have found nests in alfalfa fields, inside greenbrier clumps in mature forest, and among the branches of a fallen dead tree. Frequently they are near trails, roads, or fields, often partially hidden by low-growing plants such as honeysuckle and blueberry.

The white to buff-colored eggs, sometimes blotched with brownish spots, are deposited directly on whatever leaves or debris are present on the ground surface. The eggs measure about 2 by 2½ inches. They are laid in a slight depression made by the weight of the hen's body and perhaps shaped by scratching. In some states the hens reportedly have covered their eggs with leaves or bark (Ligon; Hillestad, 1970; Schorger, 1966). Roger Latham said that some hens will place leaves on their backs while they incubate; later, when they leave to feed, the leaves fall off onto the eggs.

A typical nest (Williams *et al.,* 1968) was 8 inches wide and 10 inches long. Generally it contained more debris than the surrounding area, indicating that some nest material was gathered by the hen. The nest materials were items available close by, and there was no evidence that the hen went more than a few feet to collect them. Most nests were in the transition zone between oak scrub and glade. Saw palmetto and wire grass were the common plant life about the nest.

Rio Grande turkeys choose nesting sites among wild peach, sand plum, mesquite, lantana, prickly pear, grasses, or forbs. Tom Logan found their nests are often on brushy hillsides, eroded ravine banks, or in alfalfa fields (personal communication). Merriam's turkeys often nest in areas without low-growing vegetation (Ligon), sometimes against a tree trunk.

After she begins to incubate her eggs, the hen's movements are very restricted. Florida turkey hens seldom leave the nest during incubation for more than two hours (Williams *et al.,* 1968). Usually they leave briefly to feed in midmorning or midafternoon. They frequently fly to and from the nest, since by taking wing and alighting a few feet from it they make it more difficult for predators to track them to the nest. The behavior of hens of other turkey subspecies is very similar.

The eggs have an opportunity to air while the hen is feeding. Carbon dioxide which has accumulated near the shell surface can then clear away. This airing helps ensure normal development of the embryo. The hen may also turn her eggs, thus preventing the embryo from sticking to one side of the inner wall.

Incubation and brooding are strictly the hen's job. She incubates the eggs for twenty-seven to twenty-eight days. If she is disturbed in the first few days of incubation, she may abandon the nest. During the late stages of incubation she is reluctant to leave the nest and will allow humans to approach much closer than previously. When eggs

A Merriam's turkey nest at the base of a ponderosa pine (U.S. Forest Service).

are destroyed or when the hen deserts the nest, she will usually renest elsewhere. However, when her poults are killed after hatching, there is no evidence that the hen attempts to renest.

If we were to open an egg at the end of the first day of incubation, we would see only the primitive spinal cord (Marsden and Martin). Leg parts, ear holes, neck, eyes, and a beaklike structure are visible by the eighth day. At the end of two weeks the body of the chick embryo is nearly covered with feathers, the preen gland is present, the beak is hardened, and claws have formed. By the twenty-sixth day the embryo is fully developed and the yolk sac is inside the unhatched chick's body.

Incubation may be interrupted at any time by predators, flooding, wildfire, operations of farm equipment, or desertion. Usually only the eggs are destroyed, but occasionally the hen is killed as well. Bobcats and foxes are predators of nesting hens. A dead hen was once found on the nest where she had been bitten by a water moccasin. The proportion of successful nests varies from year to year and area to area. Between 20 and 60 percent of the nests produce poults.

One Rio Grande turkey nested in this islandlike grass clump within a washout (U.S. Fish and Wildlife Service).

Spring

Yearling hens have been known to produce some large broods. Wayne Bailey (1964), trapping in West Virginia, captured five large broods in 1963 which were led by yearling hens. Of the broods he captured these were among the largest. In ten years of trapping, that was the first year he observed yearling hens that contributed substantially to production. C. R. Watts (1972) and Williams *et al.* (1971), however, found that yearling hens made a significant contribution to production.

Severe weather influences hatching success and poult survival. For example, in southeastern Montana, 81 percent of the poults are normally produced from nests in which incubation starts before May 10. In 1967, the area had a thirty-seven-inch snowfall on May 1. Precipitation during May and June was two and a half times above normal. That year production of young turkeys was below normal, and only 16 percent of the poults were from nests in which incubation had started before May 10.

Because turkeys lay their eggs on the ground, many animals that like eggs discover them and eat them. Raccoons, skunks, opossums, snakes, crows, ravens, dogs, coyotes, bears, minks, ground squirrels, cotton rats, ringtails (the bassariscus of the Southwest), and foxes are among the nest predators. Free-ranging hogs, once common in the South, are no longer important nest predators. The European wild hogs of Tennessee, North Carolina, Florida, California, and Texas are opportunists and will eat the eggs in nests occasionally, but their ability to locate nests does not appear to be any better than that of the more common predators (Henry).

Floods sometimes are a hazard to turkeys nesting in bottomlands. Rapidly melting snow or hard rains, upstream, swell the rivers until they overflow and cover nests in low spots.

The patience of some hens is finally rewarded when their eggs begin hatching. The poult, struggling within the egg, cuts around the inside of one end with its egg tooth, a small pointed growth on the top of the bill. (The egg tooth drops off soon after hatching.) This process of the chick breaking or cutting cleanly through some of the shell is called pipping. The clean cut around the ends of eggs from which poults have successfully hatched is easily distinguished from the roughly broken eggshells left by predators.

Biologists in Ohio (Donohoe *et al.*, 1968) observed an Eastern wild turkey hen during the late stages of incubation. The day before her eggs hatched she was apparently on the nest continuously for 19½ hours and then left for only 77 minutes. Her first hatched poult was seen at the nest edge at 11 A.M. the following day, and she fed it, still sitting on the nest, by picking up material she could reach without getting up and then placing it in the poult's mouth. At 2:20 P.M. the observers saw five poults moving about the nest. The hen and her poults remained at the nest until 9:15 A.M. the next morning; then she led them away.

Twenty-four to forty-eight hours elapse between the time the chicks begin pipping the eggs and the time that the hen leads her poults from the nest. In the Ohio observation, 22¾ hours elapsed from the time the first poult was seen until the hen led the poults away. In a nest in Florida there were 46 hours between the time three eggs were ob-

The opossum is another nest predator.   *The raven eats turkey eggs.*

served pipping and the time when the hen departed with ten poults. Robert Wheeler once found a nest at 9:00 A.M. with two poults, one pipped egg, and five other eggs; 24 hours later the hen was seen a hundred feet from the nest with eight poults.

The movements of the broods are fairly limited during the first hours after they leave the nest. One brood moved as much as 151 yards per hour during parts of its first day away from the nest, stopping and resting for long periods. A study of young broods in Florida indicated the average distance from the nest to their first night's roost was only 212 yards (Williams *et al.,* 1972*a*). The hens led the poults from the border between oak scrub and saw palmetto flats where the nests were located into cypress forest. They stayed there for several weeks and did not move more than a few yards from concealing plant life. After they learned to fly, the poults frequented fields and glades farther from dense vegetation in which they could hide.

Radiotelemetry equipment was used to follow four hens immediately after their broods hatched. The broods roosted on the ground

Wild turkey poults hatching from a nest in Alabama (Sydney Johnson).

Turkey poults are precocial and leave the nest with the hen soon after hatching (Lovett Williams).

for the first eleven or twelve nights after leaving the nest. Before the poults learned to fly they roosted beneath the mother's body, outstretched wings, and tail. The hen selected a spot in a cypress grove at the base of a tree stump or cypress knee. The amount of low plant life providing concealment for the roosting birds varied from none to fairly heavy vegetation. They did not roost in thickets or dense shrubbery, although it was usually available nearby.

Soon after hatching, the poults are moving about, finding some of their own food. During the first hours they rely for energy on the absorbed yolk sac in their bodies. They peck indiscriminately at small objects and bright spots which contrast with the ground, learning what is edible by experience.

However, they still depend on the hen's body for protection (North Carolina Wildlife Resources Commission).

Spring

At hatching, the poults have well-developed legs and their eyes are open. A yellowish-brown down covers their bodies, and their flight feathers are just emerging. Turkeys are precocial birds (able to run about after hatching), which develop better regulation of their body temperatures than altricial birds (robins, for example) that are born blind, naked, and dependent on the parent for food. But turkey poults still depend on the protection—the warming and shielding (brooding)—that the hen provides. This is especially true during stormy or cool weather that may cause a breakdown in their temperature-regulating mechanisms, followed by death from chilling and exposure.

Robert Wheeler indicated that exposure and exhaustion, rather than predation, were the chief causes of loss during the poult's first weeks of life. According to Wheeler, a poult that survived its first six weeks had passed the period of greatest danger, and its chances for reaching adulthood were good.

A cool spring, with prolonged rains coinciding with the peak hatching period, usually results in a high mortality of young turkeys and a poor production year. The loss of young poults because of exposure usually comes when they are separated from the hen (Mosby and Handley, Ligon, Wheeler). During prolonged rains the hen is forced to stop brooding the poults in order to eat and to lead them into feeding areas. Exposure to the rain and wet vegetation can soon lead to soaked, shivering poults that weaken and cannot keep up with the hen. In such situations they are unable to maintain their proper body temperatures and soon die. Others may die in spite of the hen's brooding efforts. H. L. Blakey found a hen brooding nine poults even though all were dead as a result of a short spring shower.

The poults' heat-production ability increases from hatching until they are about fifteen days old. At the same time their feathers are providing better insulation. When plumage is fully developed and metabolic control improved, poults are less dependent on the hen for shelter from inclement weather.

53

Spring is always a busy time for turkeys. For the hen, as we have seen, there is mating, starting the nest, laying the eggs, incubating, and brood care. The male has to try to establish himself as dominant among the other males; if he succeeds, he leaves the roost early each morning and hurries off to court the ladies. He eats little or nothing at this time, and his frequent mating tapers off only when the hens begin their incubation. By then he may have lost two tail feathers to a stealthy bobcat or carry a few No. 5 lead shot, attesting to a careless moment in responding to a hunter's imitation of the hen's call. His breast sponge will be drained, as each morning he wanders in search of companionship, gobbling about over hill and dale, and finally he enters the period of the summer doldrums.

Summer

THE FIELD OF white clover is warm in the midmorning sun. Thousands of insects move unseen among the stems of the clover and grasses. Cicadas in the trees at the field's border begin to sing in the summer heat. Along the edge of the meadow the hen turkey leads her seven poults. When grasshoppers and tiny green leafhoppers fly up, the poults scurry here and there, pursuing them. Now and then one of the brood plucks a piece of green leaf or tastes a seed dropped to the ground by last year's plants. The hen picks clover leaves, then catches two grasshoppers and a caterpillar. A field sparrow sings from a tall thistle, while a nearby meadowlark sits quietly on her nest in a clump of big bluestem. One too-warm poult stops for a moment, holding its wings down and away from its body, with its bill open, and pants rapidly to lower its body temperature.

In this field and others like it the turkey hen recognizes two elements necessary for her poults' survival. Here she can bring the poults to let them dry in the sun after a rain shower in the forest. Here also is an excellent composition of foods in abundance. No other part of the habitat is as important to the young poults' welfare as these sunny fields or forest openings.

The diet during the early weeks of a young poult's life consists of insects and the green leaves of succulent plants (Wheeler, Ligon), and open areas are the best places to find these foods. Mosby's and Hand-

55

Poults find an abundance of food in clover fields.

ley's study of the foods of turkeys in Virginia showed that almost one half of all the insects eaten were grasshoppers. An additional quarter of the insects consumed were fly larvae of various species. Forest openings, or open woods with grassy and weedy undergrowth, are necessary for the production of these and other insects. Poults are led to such areas soon after hatching and continue to feed there for their first few weeks of life.

On the meadow, while one poult diverges momentarily to pluck a ripe dewberry, another moves off to one side and struts. Even the youngest poult will strut occasionally. When a behavior is stereotyped for all members of a species, it is called a species-specific or fixed-action pattern. Fixed-action patterns are apparently determined genetically (inherited), because even a young bird reared in isolation will exhibit this behavior without having seen another bird do it.

The hen pauses, momentarily alert to the flight of a passing black

Young poults sun themselves after their feathers become wet (Lovett Williams).

vulture. When a poult becomes lost in a chase after a cricket it gives the distress call *peep-peep-peep-peep,* a whistlelike note similar in sound to the call of a baby chick. The hen replies with her brood call, and when the poult returns, the reassembled group moves into a small sumac clump to rest and to dust-bathe in the sandy soil.

Turkeys dust-bathe during the warmer months, and their dusting places are generally oval-shaped depressions about the size of the bird's body and a few inches deep at the center. They are more prevalent in sandy soils where turkeys have no difficulty wallowing out a "bath" and the plant growth is slow to become re-established.

Turkeys sit in these baths and rake dirt toward the body with the bill. Then they ruffle their feathers and shake their wings, legs, and body, stirring up dust. The dust is thought to get into the breathing spiracles of mites, bird lice, and other parasites of the skin or feathers of birds and to kill them. It might also relieve the skin itching that results from molting feathers. Turkeys often dust at midday; members of the flock may have separate dusting places, often within a few feet of each other. Dusting sites are common along field borders, and turkeys may establish them under sumacs or small oaks, which provide shade and overhead protection from avian predators. Dusting places around old charred logs or burned brush piles are also heavily used.

Most poults will become adults if they survive the first few months. Brood counts indicate a gradual decrease in average brood size during the summer. In Michigan the average brood declined from 10 poults in May to 6 in August. In Tennessee the change in a typical year was from 8.1 poults in June to 6.3 in August. The losses evident in the decreasing brood size are caused by exposure, severe weather, accidents, parasites, poaching, disease, and predation.

Sometimes the growing poults are struck by cars; they also may be injured during a farmer's mowing operations or during their early flying experiences. Small poults may become entangled in thickets or fall into depressions on the ground from which they cannot escape.

A turkey dust bath.

Occasionally a poult may succumb to an ectoparasitic infection. Lyle Petersen and Arthur Richardson studied a Merriam's hen and her half-grown wild poults that were frequenting a barnyard in which there were domestic chickens. These poults acquired a bad infection of mites and lice from the chickens and one poult died as a result.

We have seen that cold spring rainfall can seriously reduce poult numbers. A shortage of rain can also be a problem in areas like southwestern Texas, where spring drought generally means a poor poult crop. The exact reason for lowered production during drought is unknown. It may be due to the reduced hatchability of eggs, and of those chicks that hatch, many may die of heat exhaustion or starvation caused by a shortage of insects and succulent grasses.

Losses caused by predators seem more dramatic; the list of animals that prey on turkeys includes hawks, owls, eagles, foxes, bobcats, coyotes, skunks, bears, opossums, dogs, weasels, house cats, and snakes. Considering the number of predators it's a wonder that more poults aren't killed. We can credit the alertness of the hen and the speed and hiding ability of the poults for the high survival rate.

The following episode illustrates how well the poults can hide and what efforts hens will make to protect their young. One afternoon

The hen is ever watchful for predators (H. L. Holbrook).

when I walked into a small field I saw two hens about two hundred feet away. One ran into the forest while the other started the broken-wing act, by which turkeys and many other ground-nesting birds lure men and animals away from their young. She flopped about and staggered into the woods. Instead of following her I started looking for her poults. When she realized her ruse had been unsuccessful she returned. Judging from her reaction I must have been close to the young birds. Spreading her wings she approached in a low crouch, in a threat display. Once she came within fifteen feet of me, and when I

The color patterns of the poult help it hide (Lovett Williams).

pretended to chase her she hissed and ran into the woods, giving the *putt,* or alarm note, loudly. Although I searched for another ten to fifteen minutes, I never did find her brood.

In 1906 Samuel Clemens commented on the hen's feigning in his humorous style: "I followed an ostensibly lame turkey over a considerable part of the United States one morning, because I believed in her and could not think she would deceive a mere boy, and one who was trusting her and considering her honest."

The cripple ruse or injury-feigning behavior is not exhibited by all hens. Biologists in Florida (Williams *et al.,* 1972*a*) observed a number of hens with poults that did not feign injury but would crouch and "freeze." If a hen was seen she stood erect, gave the alarm *putt* at one- to two-second intervals, and moved away from the poults. As she began *putt*-ing the chicks ran from beneath her and spread out over a few square yards. Poults only a few days old froze and remained motionless even when handled by one of the investigators. Eight- or nine-day-old poults attempted to hide under ground litter or plants. The disturbed hen generally moved out of sight, but she could be heard *putt*-ing rapidly. When the danger was past she returned, called to her poults, and led them away.

Poults will "freeze" in response to the hen's warning (U.S. Forest Service).

Hens are sometimes surprisingly aggressive toward predators. R. R. Johnson told of watching two hens and their poults as they were attacked by a hawk (buteo). After the hawk's first unsuccessful pass it circled and returned but was met in midair by one hen at a height of eighteen feet. The collision knocked the hawk to the ground, whereupon it flew to a tree. A hen flew toward the tree, and again the hawk dived toward the poults. This time the other hen met it in the air. The hawk retreated to the tree and was pursued. At last it left for good. Similarly, H. L. Holbrook saw an attack upon crows by hen turkeys defending poults about two weeks old.

Snakes are the only predators which turkeys have been reported to kill. Single turkeys as well as flocks have been observed attacking snakes—rattlesnakes, water moccasins, and king snakes (Beyers, Duncan, Jackson, Rutledge, Santleben). An entire flock will circle around the snake. Individual turkeys then dash forward to strike the snake with their wings or spurs.

The red and gray fox, bobcat, and coyote are probably the most significant predators of young poults, especially before the birds learn to fly.

However, they learn fast. According to research in Alabama, poults could fly for distances up to 50 feet by the time they were one week old (Hillestad, 1970), and the youngest poults observed flying in Florida were almost twelve days old. When they first began to roost in trees they chose limbs between 6 and 20 feet above the ground. Even in the trees the poults slept under the hen's outstretched wings until they were about four weeks old.

By the time turkeys are six weeks old, the wing and tail feathers are well developed and the poults are capable of long flights. Once the brood is able to fly and roost at night in trees it is much more likely to survive.

Lovett Williams and his co-workers (1972a) described the early morning behavior of young poults on the roost. He watched five hens with their broods. The groups were 30 to 80 feet apart on the lower limbs of separate cypress trees. At 6:16 A.M. the only hen in view was still sleeping, but her poults were hopping restlessly from limb to limb. At 6:30 one poult noticed the observer and gave the *putt* alarm call, but it soon resumed its restless motion and forgot the observer. At 6:32 A.M. one hen silently glided to the ground in the cypress woods four hundred feet from her roost. She was followed at about five-second intervals by four poults from the same tree. At 6:40 A.M. a second hen flew down in the same general direction, and immediately after her came eight poults. Neither hen was heard to utter the yelp. Another hen flew down at 6:42 A.M., followed by three poults. At 6:45, as one hen on the ground began calling, several more poults flew from the trees in her direction. By 7:00 the five hens and at least fifteen poults were moving rapidly away along the edge of a small clearing.

J. S. Ligon (page 40) reported Bill Felts's observations of a Merriam's turkey hen teaching her poults to fly.

She was on a north-east slope of about a 35 degree angle and she would fly to the low hanging limb of an aspen tree and call very loudly. The limb was about seven or eight feet from the ground. The poults, which are almost completely feathered, would try very hard to join the mother but would fall short and tumble as they hit the ground. After a series of loud calls by the mother and attempts by the young, they quit for approximately half an hour, when the hen, still on the same slope, flew into a pine tree about four feet off the ground. Three of the poults made it, two fell short and one did not attempt it at all.

The following day the brood was again observed and had remarkably improved their flying abilities.

Poults can swim for short distances but obviously are not well adapted for it. A swimming turkey stretches out its tail for support, holds its wings close to its body, and propels itself with the legs. Swimming is seldom necessary after the poults learn to fly. One three-to four-day-old poult attempted to escape from a man by swimming about thirty yards across a pond, but the effort was so exhausting that it was easily captured. Nevertheless, biologists in Florida noted that one- to two-day-old poults were led across creeks by hens, and the young poults swam more often than one would expect (Williams *et al.*, 1972*a*).

Occasionally hens are killed when the poults are young and yet the broods manage to survive. Wayne Bailey (1955*b*) observed such a brood from early July through the summer. However, these eight poults lacked the appropriate normal fear of man and automobiles and were not seen after early fall.

The hen turkey is frequently not alone in watching for predators and guiding the brood. After the poults are a few weeks old the brood may join other family groups, or it may be joined by one or more adult hens that have lost their broods or were unsuccessful at nesting. These hens, like matrons in waiting, accompany the brood continuously and help to watch for predators. Probably by their behavior they unintentionally teach the poults about new foods.

The more dominant hens will sometimes steal poults from other hens (Watts, 1972). Perhaps the brooding instinct is so strong in these individuals that they are not satisfied with small broods. Dominant hens seem to be older and more experienced; thus the chances for survival of the poults may be increased under their watchful eyes.

As summer progresses there is a change in poults' behavior. At first they respond only to the signals of the hen. Gradually their own senses become dominant as they learn to respond to stimuli like a circling hawk or a man (enemies) or insects (food, or prey). Like the young of other animals, turkeys learn about their environment by trial and error; a Florida observer noticed four poults gliding from their roost into a hyacinth-choked lake, apparently by mistake.

Young turkeys molt (replace) their body plumage twice during the summer. These molts are almost continuous; that is, the first will still be under way when the second starts. Molting permits an increase

An alert group of hens (California Department of Fish and Game).

in the number and size of feathers to compensate for the rapid body growth of young turkeys. The plumage present at hatching is called "natal down." It is lost during the postnatal molt that starts soon after hatching and is replaced by a coat of juvenal feathers that is mostly complete by the sixth week. The juvenal feathers are then lost

The poults learn from the hen. Note the poults' ruffled appearance during the molt (Florida Game and Fresh Water Fish Commission).

during a postjuvenal molt, and the feathers that come in to replace the juvenal are called the first winter plumage.

Male poults weigh about 1 pound when they are four weeks old and gain about 2 pounds per month for the next five months. The males grow more rapidly than the hens and at the age of six months may average 11 pounds; the hens average 7½ pounds.

Broods are seen along the borders of fields and other types of openings throughout the summer, which continue to provide insects as well as a variety of seeds and berries. Today a field may have an abundance of Florida paspalum; two weeks later wild oat grass or bristle grass may be ripe. Another opening a quarter mile away, with differing soil and moisture conditions, will support a totally different plant community and insect population. A third field, a few hundred yards from the first, may have the same soil type but may be on a north slope. There the plant and insect community is the same but the paspalum ripens two weeks later than that in the first meadow. By moving from field to field the family groups find sufficient variety and abundance of food to provide the energy their rapid growth requires.

Grasses, berries, and insects are the major foods for adult turkeys during the summer. Insects provide almost one tenth of the diet (Korschgen, 1967) and include grasshoppers, ground beetles, stinkbugs, June beetles, and snout beetles. Both the leaves and seeds of grasses are important. Bluegrass, crabgrass, panic grass, paspalum, bristle grass, wedgegrass, buckwheat, wild oat grass, tall purple top,

A hen and her brood use a forest road border as a travel way (U.S. Forest Service).

Even when her poults are larger the hen remains alert (Ken Stiebben, Kansas Fish and Game).

legumes, sheep sorrel, sedges, and other miscellaneous plant material provide more than one half of the summer diet for the Eastern turkey. Turkeys strip the seedheads from grasses by holding the stem cross-wise in the bill and pulling it sideways into the mouth. They also eat blackberries, cherries, huckleberries, wild grapes, blueberries, mushrooms, and mulberries. Acorns, black gum fruits, and dogwood berries that are left from the previous season or that begin to fall in late August provide only a small part of the diet but add important variety.

Summer

Since many foods used by turkeys in the summer grow in open, sunny places, these are good places to watch the hen and her brood, especially after a rain, when turkeys seek an open area, perhaps to avoid wet vegetation and to dry off. Biologists sometimes take advantage of this behavior to collect information on the season's poult production by counting turkeys along roads.

In June a brood usually stays in a relatively small area, but as summer progresses it becomes more mobile. By August the poults have no difficulty keeping up with the hen and can travel over a larger area.

Meanwhile, back in the forest, the gobblers, after the ecstasies of spring, go through a prolonged period of austerity. An old solitary gobbler may remain alone throughout the summer, but toms that spent the spring carousing in company with one or more male companions remain together. Sometimes these groups join with others until there are six to ten gobblers in one flock.

Summer is a period of rejuvenation for the tired gobblers. Not only must they recover their weight losses but they must also undergo a complete molt, of which feathers near dust baths and roosts are common evidence. Yearling males are the first to begin molting, and the hens are the last. Replacement of the plumage requires considerable energy. It seems appropriate that the hen, busy with motherly chores, undergoes the molt after some of the urgency of brooding is over.

The molt of adult wild turkeys requires four months to complete. It is gradual, and the ability to fly is not lost as it is among some waterfowl. The molt is under way by July, and by midautumn the turkeys are adorned with a new garb of the same style. Turkeys look the same the year around, unlike some other birds, such as male ducks which have different-colored plumage in winter and summer.

The molt begins with the shedding of some of the primary wing feathers. After several have been lost the molt moves to the side of the breast and thighs, then spreads over the breast and abdomen, down

67

the legs, over the rump, and up the back. The feathers on the back of the neck are the last to be replaced.

In late summer the males occasionally appear with flocks of poults and hens, but generally they travel with other males or alone. The gobblers seem less conspicuous at this season, as though they prefer to be secretive.

Necessary food, water, and roosting sites are within the area the turkey normally utilizes, and wildlife biologists have determined this acreage by attaching radio transmitters to turkeys, and then following their movements. During the summer, four individual gobblers in Alabama each traveled within 219 to 459 acres (Barwick and Speake). Another study in Alabama indicated that the entire year's travels, by gobblers, were confined to 600 acres or less except during the mating season (Davis). The movement of hens was smaller; they stayed within 345 acres or less except during the nesting period. All these movements encompassed less than one square mile.

Adult turkeys contend with about the same threats to life as the young poults, but they are more capable of resisting them. Like other animals, they are commonly afflicted with internal parasites. Some sixty parasites have now been identified inside or on the wild turkey. Sometimes the resulting infections are obvious; for example, tapeworms may so thoroughly fill the gut that it is a wonder any food passes through, or the intestinal wall may be inflamed from injury caused by the parasites. However, in most turkeys, parasites can be detected only with a microscope and ordinarily have no obvious effect on their host.

Our present knowledge about the effect of parasites on wild turkeys is limited. The general consensus is that most turkeys can live with many parasites. Death from parasitic infestations probably occurs only when the turkey is under simultaneous stress from other factors—disease or starvation, for example.

The most common disease to which wild turkeys are exposed is blackhead, or enterohepatitis. It is caused by a protozoan blood parasite found within another common turkey parasite, the caecal worm. An outbreak of blackhead can cause serious losses. M. L. Burget reported a flock of Merriam's turkeys which in a few months was reduced from fifty to twelve birds as a result of blackhead. The disease is most widespread during summer and early fall and is especially lethal to poults. Discoloration of the head, droopiness, loss of weight, and yellowish droppings are symptoms of blackhead.

The turkey can be infected by the caecal worm eggs or by accidental ingestion of soil or of food dirtied by sick birds that are car-

Gobblers often run to escape danger (U.S. Fish and Wildlife Service).

riers (birds that are infected but survive). Chickens and bobwhite quail (Kellogg and Reid) become infected but are not highly susceptible to the disease and therefore also act as carriers; poultry manure spread on fields provides a source of infection for wild turkeys. This is one reason why well-meaning landowners are seriously endangering the welfare of wild flocks when they put out food for them near their ranch headquarters on which there are poultry.

Fowl pox, fowl cholera, botulism, Newcastle disease, fowl typhoid, avian tuberculosis, aspergillosis, coccidiosis, leucocytozoon, trichomoniasis, and others are among the diseases of caged or penned turkeys. Some of these diseases have been reported in free-living wild turkeys; others are significant to turkeys only in unsanitary conditions where the birds are kept in close confinement.

The adult wild turkey is threatened by much the same predators as the poults. The larger predators—bobcats, foxes, and coyotes—are capable of overpowering a gobbler; however, losses of healthy adult turkeys to predators are uncommon. Turkeys are remarkably strong and fast and do a good job of keeping away from their enemies.

Turkeys will often run from danger rather than fly, unless they are startled by a predator close upon them. This is especially true of large gobblers, which seem to avoid the effort required to get into the air. They also seem reluctant to flush when pursued in woods where numerous branches overhead make flying difficult. The running stride of a frightened gobbler may be as much as four feet, and their running speed is about 15 to 18 miles per hour (Mosby and Handley). With a step like that, it is obvious that turkeys can cover ground quickly.

On the other hand, turkeys are strong fliers as well. With a few running steps an alarmed turkey springs into the air, and its powerful wings lift it quickly from the ground. It rises at a sharp angle and can clear the top of a sixty-foot tree when flushed within a hundred feet of the base (Mosby and Handley). It dodges densely patterned limbs with surprising agility.

If hard pressed, however, they will fly into trees (Michigan Department of Natural Resources).

Turkeys are generally not long-distance fliers, although a gobbler flew 2¼ miles across Lake Texhoma, Oklahoma. The average flight to escape danger is only a few hundred yards. However, in mountainous areas the birds may fly to the next ridge or glide as much as a mile with only intermittent wingbeats. An individual bird will become exhausted if it is flushed repeatedly. For example, hunters flushed one gobbler three times in rapid succession. The third time the bird flew only half a mile then fell exhausted in a river.

Turkeys are capable of extremely rapid takeoffs in spite of their large size. F. L. Poole studied the relationship between the area of bird's wings and total body weight. He used a ratio of 1.0 or larger to indicate a large wing surface in comparison to body weight. The Eastern wild turkey has a ratio of 0.962, which ranks it with other birds with a fast takeoff like the ruffed grouse (1.02) and mallard

Turkeys can fly 55 miles an hour (Max Hamilton, Indiana Department of Conservation).

(0.77). Most large birds have a lower ratio and less initial takeoff speed, like the Canada goose (0.50) and mute swan (0.59). Poole also measured the area covered by a turkey hen's outspread wings. They covered 3,752 square centimeters (about 4 square feet), compared to 2,820 for the Canada goose and 4,156 for whistling swans. With this much wing surface it's obvious that turkeys have a lot of lifting power.

The flight speed of a wild gobbler has been clocked on an automobile speedometer at 55 miles per hour over a distance of one mile (Kanoy). Henry Mosby and Charles Handley calculated the speed of flight using a stopwatch and pacing. A gobbler flushed from the edge of a field averaged 42.8 miles per hour. Two half-grown hens were clocked at 32.5 miles per hour at a time when neither of them appeared to be particularly alarmed.

Turkeys are relatively fast in comparison with other species. The

72

mallard has been clocked at 40 miles per hour (Cottam *et al.*), the pintail duck at 49, ruffed grouse at 51 (Edminster), Canada geese at 26, sandhill cranes at 40, and mourning doves at 70 miles per hour.

Nevertheless, turkeys do not spend much time flying. Most of their traveling is on foot. Their daily trip a few hundred feet to and from the roost is their only regular flight. In spring, Rio Grande turkeys sometimes fly from the roost to their courting grounds, and hens may fly to and from the nest. During periods of deep snow turkeys sometimes fly as much as a mile to feeding areas, and in winter they may also fly into trees to feed on the buds, but generally they are ground dwellers.

Combined with their good physical escape abilities is their sharp eyesight. Man's acuteness of vision is about equal to that of birds, but the ability to note detail in the entire field of vision is much better in birds. Thus their vision, if no better, is considerably faster than that of man. "A bird with a single glance lasting perhaps a second," according to R. J. Pumphrey, "takes in a picture which a man could accumulate only by laboriously scanning the whole field piece by piece with the most accurate portion of his retina" (page 58). Turkeys don't have the binocular vision of owls, for example (which gives depth perception in pursuit of prey), because their eyes are positioned on the side of the head. The eye position of turkeys is important to them because it permits vision in a greater circumference (300 degrees), thereby making them more aware of their surroundings. However, turkeys see a flat picture that does not give them dimensional information useful for judging distances. They judge distance by moving the head slightly and taking several glances.

Birds' eyes apparently have a lower threshhold (greater sensitivity) in detecting movement than human eyes. Pumphrey thought that a bird might be able to tell that a clock was going by looking at the hour hand, just as a man would discover changes in the position of the minute hand. This ability to perceive very small movements, plus the wide field of vision, makes the wild turkey's eyesight one of its best defenses.

Paul Sturkie reported that all birds active in the daytime have color vision. Turkeys show evidence of detecting the momentary color changes in the head adornments of gobblers and can distinguish between grains of white and yellow corn, though in either case they might be recognizing shades of black and white rather than color differences. However, perception of color in birds is thought to be as good as ours, if not better. In fact, they may be able to improve on man's ability to discriminate mixed or pigmentary colors. The colored oil droplets in the cones of birds' eyes are believed to be intraocular color filters that give birds a power of discrimination man can achieve only with extra-ocular color filters (Pumphrey). It would certainly be sad if the hen couldn't appreciate the beautiful colors reflected from the male plumage.

Turkeys cannot see well in the dark. If they are disturbed on moonlit nights they can maneuver and fly to a safer roost, but on dark nights they fly reluctantly, their wings beating against branches.

Turkeys also use their sense of hearing to good advantage. Their ears are sensitive to frequencies of 200 to 6,000 cycles or more (Schleidt), although they apparently can detect more subtle variations of frequency than the human ear and respond quicker. Whatever the season or daily activity, they seem to be aware of a very great range of sounds in their environment. Once when I was photographing turkeys from a blind, the clicking noise as I rewound the film was enough to send them running.

The ease with which a gobbler can locate a calling hen attests to the turkey's good hearing. Perhaps it is not unusual for a bird familiar with its environment, but I am still amazed by its accuracy. A gobbler hearing only one or two yelps from a hen, several hundred yards to a quarter of a mile away, under varying wind conditions in hilly topography, still seems to know exactly from where the hen called. At best

I spend half my time trying to figure where the gobbler is, but one or two imitations of the hen's yelp has brought him straight to my blind, where he may stand around for ten minutes gobbling.

Observations of turkeys indicate that their sense of smell is not highly developed. If a man is well hidden, turkeys will approach downwind to within a few feet of him without detecting his presence. Furthermore, the olfactory lobes of the brain are relatively small.

Turkeys may have a sense of taste (in the strict sense) equivalent to that of man. The general consensus is that many birds can distinguish sweet, sour, salty, and bitter (Portmann). Turkeys are capable of identifying and avoiding some drugs with which they have had previous experience; however, it is possible that this identification could be based on some sense other than taste. Verne E. Davison felt that taste, rather than color, attracts birds to certain foods. He offered birds a

Turkeys have good eyesight but lack binocular vision because of the eye's position on the side of the head (Texas Parks and Wildlife Department).

choice of a large variety of seeds, altering the colors of certain highly preferred seeds with cake coloring. The birds selected these in spite of the color change. Likewise the low-preference seeds were not eaten more readily when their colors were changed. Surface texture, shape, and size did not seem to influence choice.

Like people, turkeys have a place—the trees—to escape from all, or almost all, the troubles of the day. Three predators that might occasionally take a roosting turkey are the bobcat, the raccoon, and the horned owl. Owls appear to be the most effective of the three. Turkeys have sensory organs in the legs called corpuscles of Herbst, which detect vibrations through the surface the bird stands on. They are especially effective when the bird is on the roost in a resting posture. Vibrations along the branch can warn a roosting turkey of the approach of a bobcat or raccoon.

Each evening the turkeys arrive at an appropriate roosting place soon after sundown. They leave the ground when the light begins to get so dim that further delay might put their lives in danger from ground predators. Roosting sometimes includes a running start from the ground, then flight from a hillside, followed by a glide into the tree. Frequently there are subsequent shifts to different limbs or other trees before the birds find the appropriate spot and settle down for the night.

When wild turkeys sleep, they relax the neck and rest the head on the breast. At other times they tuck the head under a wing. As they relax and bend their legs, the feet automatically tighten around the limb, so they don't have to worry about losing their grip while sleeping.

At daybreak, about thirty minutes before sunrise, the birds awaken, stretch their wings and feathers, shake themselves, preen, call, and sometimes even gobble from the roost. When it is light enough to permit flight they glide down from the roost and land in a small opening among the trees. Roosts are discoverable by the groups of droppings and molted feathers on the ground, near them, or by the sight or sounds of birds going to or leaving the roost. The swishing wingbeats can be heard for several hundred yards on a quiet evening. In exceptionally good roosts the droppings may accumulate to depths of twelve to fourteen inches in spots (Burget). More typical is a clumping of several dozen droppings, in various stages of decay, scattered in a radius of a few feet.

I have seen turkeys roosting in many different places: in oaks within narrow ravines on the Cumberland Plateau in Tennessee; in cypress trees over sloughs bordering the Mississippi River; in oaks in the Cross-timbers of Oklahoma; in cottonwoods in western Oklahoma; and in oaks and pines in Michigan. Turkeys seem to have rather subtle preferences for roost locations. Sometimes they use the same spot several nights in succession, or with no apparent pattern; on other occasions a roost may be only one of several used.

In southern coastal and river bottomland areas turkeys often roost in large cypress trees growing in the water, a roost situation commonly interpreted as a selection that might discourage a bobcat or some other tree-climbing predator from reaching them.

Usually Merriam's turkeys prefer overmature ponderosa pine, but they also use old Engelmann spruce, narrow-leaf cottonwood, and white fir (Hoffman, 1968). The average diameter of fifty-two roost

The raccoon is occasionally a daytime occupant of trees where turkeys roost at night (North Carolina Wildlife Resources Commission).

Cypress trees are used for roosting in the South (U.S. Forest Service).

trees at breast height was 22.5 inches, and the trees averaged 65 feet high. The turkeys chose trees sheltered from the wind and selected the tallest and largest tree on the site, probably because of the shape and openness of the crown. Roosting areas with a forest clearing or with an open ridge nearby were also preferred, apparently for ease of takeoff and landing.

Regardless of the exact roost circumstances, wild turkeys are safer sleeping in trees than on the ground. Theoretically this ground-dwelling bird, sometime in the distant past, began roosting in trees, and because it was a behavioral adaptation with survival advantage, it has persisted ever since.

A roosting site of Merriam's turkeys in ponderosa pine (U.S. Fish and Wildlife Service).

Fall and Winter

FALL IS PROBABLY our universal choice as the favorite season. The oppressive summer heat is past. The larder is full after harvest. Now comes a pause before the impact of winter winds and snows. No matter where we live, we share part of the beautiful color change which is most dramatic in the deciduous forests of the eastern United States. The reds of sumac and the yellows of poplar and aspen, contrasting with the deep greens of pine and the reds of maple and oak, daub hillsides like spots on a painter's palette.

Fall is a restful period for turkeys. Gone is the urgency of mating and the demands of caring for poults. In early September, nuts and acorns are beginning to fall or have been knocked loose by squirrels, woodpeckers, and blue jays. The days grow shorter and the nights cooler. Soon the first hard frost comes. On the following morning at daybreak one can sit and watch the steady downward drift of leaves falling to the forest floor.

At this season all races of turkeys may be seen in flocks containing adult hens, poults, and occasionally a few gobblers; however, the gobblers usually remain segregated in smaller flocks. Turkeys now spend more time in the woods. With cool weather the variety of food in fields diminishes as insects and plants become dormant. While food is still abundant turkeys may stay within a hundred acres for several weeks. Their daily movements will increase if acorns are scarce, and they may then travel over several square miles (1,280 to 2,560 acres).

A hard spring frost, while oaks are flowering, results in a smaller acorn crop; however, not all oaks are affected—some flower later or grow in places not subjected to frost. An added insurance against a complete lack of acorns is the difference in time required for the acorns of different oaks to mature. Pollinated flowers in the white oak group—post, white, and chestnut, for example—develop into mature acorns within five to six months. In the red oak group—red, black, blackjack, and so on—it requires eighteen months. Thus a total failure of the acorn crop is unlikely, but a diminished crop will influence the choices of turkeys in where they spend the winter and in how far they move each day.

Larry Barwick and Dan Speake, in Alabama, determined that during the fall the average movements of six gobblers covered slightly more than 400 acres. In Virginia, Jack Raybourne found that four birds ranged over 550 acres during a four-week period and, within this acreage, moved an average of 1.7 miles each day.

The same habitat is often used by turkeys through the fall and winter. For Rio Grande turkeys the first movement from the summer to the winter range begins as early as August. Most birds move together in family groups. The combined winter flock is not formed until later, and its formation is stimulated by the first bad weather.

Fall feeding by turkeys is leisurely. They scrape the leaves backward first with one foot and then the other, then pause to pick up any exposed tidbits before scratching some more. The manner of scratching by an individual turkey leaves a cleared patch in the leaves, roughly pyramidal in shape, with the peak pointing in the direction the bird is traveling. The speed of movement during feeding varies from several hundred yards to half a mile an hour. Tomorrow, or a few days later, the birds will probably travel this same route again.

Turkeys have two main feeding periods, the first few hours after they leave the roost and the last few hours before sunset, but they may feed sparingly at any time of the day. In summer, however, when it is hot and the poults must rest more, broods spend midday loafing, sometimes among the trees bordering an opening. During the fall and winter, the family groups seem to be on the move throughout the day.

Crabgrass seeds are abundant along woodland trails and field borders and are an important fall food of the Eastern turkey. Acorns, beechnuts, pecans, hackberries, cherries, dogwood berries, hawthorn and black gum fruits, and other mast are the most abundant foods at this season. Insects provide up to 10 percent of the diet. Late-maturing grasses and weeds—smartweed, wild rye, paspalum, purple-top, panic grass, and sheep sorrel—are eaten by turkeys and they may glean corn, wheat, and rye seeds from waste left in harvested fields. In fall, the young shoots of winter wheat and rye provide them with greens.

Hickory nuts and hard-shelled pecans are occasionally eaten by wild turkeys (Glover; Good and Webb; Martin *et al.;* Meanley; L. G. Webb). Hickory nuts comprised 2.9 percent of the diet of wild turkeys in Alabama (Webb, 1941). One would not suspect that something as hard as a hickory nut would be suitable food, especially when it is swallowed

The feet are useful for "scratching," fighting, and clinging to the roost.

whole. But the turkey's gizzard (muscular stomach) is an efficient grinding machine. A. W. Schorger (1960) found that although it required up to 79 pounds of pressure to crush pecans, these were broken after remaining in the gizzard for only one hour; hickory nuts required about 30 hours. Schorger was studying domestic birds; the nuts may be broken up faster in wild turkeys accustomed to eating hard foods.

Disintegration of nuts in the gizzard is entirely mechanical. Hickory nuts are not broken down at the suture as one would expect. First they are worn by grit in the gizzard until a small cavity forms in the shell. Then it breaks under the pressure exerted by the gizzard wall.

The foods eaten in the fall by Merriam's and Rio Grande turkeys differ from those of the Eastern turkey, especially in the smaller amounts of acorns and nuts consumed. Grass seeds, insects, and green forage are more important for the Rio Grande turkey. Merriam's turkeys feed on many fleshy fruits, ponderosa pine seeds, seeds of grasses, and insects (Twedt). The diversity of foods found in one turkey's crop was truly amazing. A Merriam's hen collected (shot) in February had eaten 76 alligator-bark juniper berries, 25 piñon nuts, 6 acorns, and 30 inch-long worms, as well as green grass blades and gravel for grit (Ligon).

Turkeys share their harvest of nature's bounty with other forest

White-tailed deer are common in most areas where turkeys live.

The ruffed grouse is a forest neighbor of the wild turkey and eats many of the same foods (Georgia Game and Fish Commission).

occupants. Robins, starlings, and cedar waxwings like hackberries. Robins and grouse delight in eating grapes, which turkeys also eat. Quail, grouse, deer, wild hogs, squirrels, mice, rats, and chipmunks feed heavily on acorns. Wood ducks and mallards feed on acorns and beechnuts in places near water. Crows, blackbirds, cowbirds, sparrows, meadowlarks, grackles, mourning doves, quail, ducks, and geese all compete with turkeys for grain crops. The most competitive are those birds that group in large flocks from late summer until spring. Texas ranchers complain about huge flocks of robins that move in during December and "clean out" all the berries on their land. Blackbirds, starlings, cowbirds, and cedar waxwings appear in equally impressive flocks and eat large amounts of grain or fruits.

The bobwhite quail is another neighbor (Oklahoma Department of Wildlife Conservation).

Generally, in spite of competition for food, there is enough for all wildlife. Chufa, or nut grass, is naturally abundant in parts of the eastern United States and the coastal plains. There is usually enough for raccoons, deer, wild hogs, sandhill cranes, ducks, and turkeys. This grass has small nutlike tubers on the roots, which turkeys learn to scratch out once they become aware of them through the rooting of wild hogs or the digging of raccoons. The plant grows well on light soils where turkeys can unearth them easily. Chufa has been planted specifically for turkeys in the Piedmont region of the Southeast.

By early fall, adult wild turkeys have nearly completed their summer molt, and the young turkeys are undergoing the molt into their first winter feathers. This partial molt begins about twelve to fourteen weeks after hatching and is the first to indicate sex differences in young turkeys. The breast and back feathers of the toms now have black tips, and the hens, buff. At about fifteen weeks of age the two central pairs of tail feathers are replaced, but the remaining tail feathers are retained until the following summer. The new central pair of tail feathers, much longer than the rest, is one of the means of distinguishing a yearling wild turkey from an adult.

As a flock moves through the woods there are always some members

Ready to retreat (Ted Borg, South Carolina Wildlife Resources Department).

on the alert for natural predators or man. Although turkeys are less vocal at this season than during the gobbling period, they are far from being "bill-tied."

Most people are not aware of the wide variety of noises a turkey can make. I had observed turkeys for several years and thought I was familiar with all their calls but I heard some that were new to me one crisp morning at daybreak. I was deer hunting and had walked to my stand with the aid of a flashlight and compass. As the presunrise light began to filter through the trees, I could hear turkeys stirring on a roost nearby. The first calls were familiar, but these progressed into such a great variety of chirps and squeaks that I couldn't imagine what else had joined the turkeys. It turned out that there were no mysterious intruders; all the noises were made by about thirty Eastern turkeys as they readied themselves for the day.

Latham (1956) listed six basic types of calls: the cluck, the alarm *putt* or *pert,* the yelp, the whistle or *kee-kee* of the very young poult, the guttural roost call or tree yelp, and the gobble of the mature male. In addition, there are five types of yelps, three types of clucks, and trills, all with sex, age, and individual variations in sound.

The yelp is descriptively written as *keouk.* The hen's notes are in a close sequence—*keouk-keouk-keouk*—while the gobbler's are more drawn out—*keouk . . . keouk . . . keouk*—and can sometimes be mistaken for a small dog barking at a distance. The old gobbler is seldom heard yelping. When he does, it is a deep coarse note. The guttural roost call is a coarse, muffled yelp with the notes drawn out longer than in other types of yelping.

The cluck is used as an assembly note or as a means of questioning. This short, sharp note is best described as *hut.* Many a wary gobbler, yelped almost to within gun range, has been reassured with a cluck. The warning *putt,* a call with which all hunters soon become familiar, is the note that precedes flight from danger. It is similar to the cluck but higher-pitched and shorter.

85

The trill, a rolling call, is used in several situations. A high-pitched trill is part of the threat display which precedes fighting. When low-pitched, the trill seems to be a sign of recognition as one turkey approaches another. The trill and *kut* may be combined if highly desirable food is found.

By late fall the young toms weigh 12 to 14 pounds and the young hens 6 to 8½ pounds. Now, as the young toms become as large or larger than the adult hens, apparently some conflict in interest develops. Perhaps the adult hen views the young male as a threat to her higher position in the dominance order; often she begins to peck and to chase him. At any rate, by late fall the young gobbler may be driven from the flock (Hillestad, 1970; Watts, 1972), generally around the time of winter flock formation. The young tom is accompanied by his sibling mates. They may join others to form flocks of young gobblers; occasionally they are accepted into a flock of older males. The young hens remain secure in their flock association with the adult hens. In some areas, however, young gobblers stay with the hens all winter and are not on their own until early spring.

In western Oklahoma, part of a winter flock of Merriam's turkeys formed in late October. At this time about 60 percent of the birds were still not present, and additional birds continued to join the main

Rio Grande turkeys feeding through rangeland. Flocks composed only of gobblers are common during fall and winter (Texas Parks and Wildlife Department).

flock throughout the winter. Peak numbers are generally not reached before early February.

Ordinarily the sexes are segregated into separate flocks throughout the winter, the hen flocks being composed of birds of all ages. But even where separation of sexes is common, yearling gobblers or an occasional adult may sometimes be found with flocks of hens. In Montana, Robert Jonas found (1964) that winter flocks of mixed sexes were the rule rather than the exception.

Winter flocks of Rio Grande turkeys in Oklahoma and Texas may number up to 500 birds; those of the other subspecies are usually smaller, seldom more than 40 to 50 birds for the Eastern wild turkey, for example.

During the winter, the movements of turkeys may increase as food diminishes and wider foraging is required to find proper nutrition. In Alabama, the ranging of gobblers increased from slightly over 400 acres during the fall to about 700 acres in the winter (Barwick and Speake). In Montana, the winter range of Merriam's turkeys included 640 to 1,280 acres (two square miles) or more (Jonas, 1964). In Oklahoma the winter range covered areas from 507 acres (Logan, personal communication) to 1,211 acres (C. H. Thomas, 1955). In Texas, winter ranges averaged 3,145 acres (J. W. Thomas *et al.,* 1972*b*).

The wintering grounds of Merriam's turkey may be 4 to 40 miles from the summer brood-rearing area (Ligon; Jonas, 1964). The Rio Grande turkey also has winter and spring ranges that are widely separated. When biologists in Texas and Oklahoma captured turkeys on their winter range and placed colored markers and leg bands on the birds, marked birds were seen 3 to 26 miles away during the late spring (J. W. Thomas *et al.,* 1966; Logan, personal communication). These wide travels differ sharply from those of the Eastern turkey, which seldom moves more than 3 miles between its winter and summer range (Barwick and Speake, Ellis and Lewis, Hillestad, 1970).

Turkeys usually return to the same winter and summer range each year, but there are exceptions. In subsequent seasons a Merriam's hen in Montana was seen on three different summer ranges and two different winter ranges (Jonas, 1964).

For both the Merriam's and Rio Grande turkey, the long distance to winter range represents an adaptive move to more suitable winter habitats. Many Merriam's turkeys spend the summer in the mountains at elevations of 6,000 to 10,000 feet; then they move downward to lower places for the winter.

In Oklahoma, three main factors seem to determine the quality of the winter range and the number of turkeys using it. Tom Logan (personal communication) reported that these factors were adequate roost sites, large quantities of available food crops, and limited human access. Large cottonwood groves were frequently the traditional winter roost. When these elements occurred together in agricultural areas, the local crops provided a substantial part of the turkey's diet.

Characteristics of winter roosts have been studied in a number of states. American elms were the common roost tree for Rio Grande turkeys in north-central Oklahoma, providing almost one half of the roosting sites. Black willow, sycamore, and cottonwood were also used for this purpose. Turkeys chose the larger trees along streams for roosting; the average tree was almost two feet in diameter and had large horizontal branches suitable for perching (Crockett). As many as twenty-four turkeys roosted in one tree. The average perch was thirty-six feet above the ground.

In western Texas, the main roost trees are cottonwoods. The same winter roosts are generally used year after year; many landowners report the trees have been used by turkeys ever since man first homesteaded the area. The birds occupy the same roost all winter unless they are disturbed. Merriam's turkeys in Montana also tended to restrict roosting to one site during winter (Jonas, 1964). In Michigan the Eastern turkeys did not return to the same roost night after night. In eastern Texas, the turkeys are also less regular in their use of a single

A cottonwood roost site used by Rio Grande turkey.

roost, apparently partly because of human disturbance.

I was unable to distinguish any increased use of conifers as roosting sites during cold or windy weather in Michigan. Both oaks and pines were used for roosting in winter and summer alike. During a blizzard in the daytime I saw turkeys roosting low in the hardwoods in the lee of a hill. Apparently they roosted there for protection from the wind. The lowest bird was only seven feet from the ground.

A decrease in light intensity stimulates turkeys to roost. Tom Logan (personal correspondence) reported that Rio Grande turkeys in Oklahoma went to roost fifteen to twenty minutes before sunset from early January until mid-March. From mid-April until mid-June, when the sun is higher on the horizon, they stayed on the ground as long as forty minutes after sunset.

Roosting is quite a ritual for a flock of wild turkeys and deserves description. On the cold late winter evening I shall describe, sunset was at 6:30 P.M. I could hear the flock of fifty or sixty Rio Grande turkeys calling and gobbling. By 6:45 the light was fading and already getting too dim for photography. Then I could see them approaching across a pasture, silhouetted against the western sky. The feeding and chasing was over. They were all alert. One nervously flapped her wings. They moved forward a few steps, then stopped and looked. After a minute's pause they again moved forward, still alert. One clucked a few times. Then a hen began running along the sloping hillside, her strong wings flapping in unison. As she left the ground the only sound was the air being swept aside with her wingbeats. Up she rose, dodging and twisting among tree limbs until, with a thrashing of her wing feathers against the small branches, she settled on her favorite roosting limb thirty feet up in a large cottonwood. *Cluck-cluck* she called to the other turkeys as they waited silently, still appraising the situation.

In a moment another hen broke away from the group and after a few steps catapulted herself into the air. She chose an elm to settle in. On they came, usually one at a time but sometimes two in the air at once. Their wingbeats dominated all other night sounds. Most of the turkeys clucked after landing and stretched their necks as though looking for danger. First they would face one direction, then another. Soon five of them sat just above me, their dark bodies gray outlines against the evening sky. One landed too close to another turkey, was pecked and pursued out toward the end of a branch, and finally relinquished the limb to the more dominant hen and flew to an adjacent tree.

In ten minutes every turkey had taken to the trees. They were

Graceful in flight despite its size (John Hall, Vermont Fish and Game Department).

Turkeys are capable of surviving lengthy periods of severe winter weather (Michigan Department of Natural Resources).

The fruiting head of sumac is a valuable winter food in areas of deep snow.

scattered up and down the hollow in cottonwoods, elms, burr oaks, and sycamores. The symphony of rushing wings, clucks, and thrashing branches was over for this evening. Occasionally a bird would change positions and flap a few feet to another branch. Three young gobblers roosted together on one limb in a tree with several hens. As if in acknowledgment of the dominant male's gobbling in the next tree, the young gobblers would occasionally fan their tail feathers. A horned owl announced its presence in the next hollow, and as I slipped away I heard a chorus of yapping coyotes.

Turkeys are very adaptable to cold weather, as I found when I spent a winter watching them in southwestern Michigan. One day cirrus clouds built up, and soon I was engulfed in a swirling world of white. The flock of eleven Eastern turkeys I had been watching were now more difficult to follow. A thin blanket of snow clung to their backs, evidence of the good insulating qualities of their feathers. They faced the wind so that cold air would not blow under their feathers. For a time they fed hurriedly in a large clump of staghorn sumac, plucking seeds from the fruiting heads. Turkeys are like other wild animals in their apparent ability to anticipate severe weather. Before a bad storm they seem more active and feed intensely as though preparing for a later period of short rations. Although sumac seeds

Wild turkey will feed where deer have pawed back the snow.

European wild hogs also root up food for turkeys (Tennessee Game and Fish Commission).

do not look palatable, they are fairly nutritious—one sample contained 7 percent protein and 17 percent fat—and are a common winter food for turkeys in southwestern Michigan.

At this time the snow had been 26 inches deep for a month, with temperatures as low as 17 degrees below zero Fahrenheit, but the turkeys were showing no harmful effects. A surprising amount of food—greenbrier berries and leaves, white pine needles, bittersweet berries, jack-pine seeds, moss, and grapes—was still available above the snow. Both turkeys and ruffed grouse took advantage of the feeding of white-tailed deer. Where deer had pawed back the snow, they found acorns, dogwood berries, legume seeds, black locust seeds, and insects lying dormant among the litter.

In addition to feeding after deer, turkeys in the southern Appalachian mountains will look for food where wild hogs have rooted. This

The "bread" of life for the Eastern wild turkey.

93

is an example of how one animal can benefit from another and a reason why the presence of many species makes for a healthier and more stable animal community.

Acorns are the most important part of the winter diet for the Eastern wild turkey. In Michigan, acorns accounted for 69 percent of the winter food and also predominated in the winter diet in Alabama, Missouri, Pennsylvania, and Virginia. One category of turkey foods that has received very little attention is what might be termed subterranean foods. These lie about one-half inch below the leaf litter and include the tubers of spring beauty and dog's-tooth violet. They grow in abundance in the northern hardwood forests of maple, beech, and cherry and provide as much as 204 pounds of food per acre. They are especially important when there is a mast failure (Hayden, 1965).

Other important foods are grasses and sedges, corn, wild grapes, dogwood berries, ferns, mosses, beechnuts, honeysuckle berries and leaves, greenbrier, poison ivy berries, and panic grasses. Piñon nuts, juniper berries, and seeds of grama grass are important winter foods for the Merriam's turkey (Levon; Reeves and Swank). Rio Grande turkeys eat acorns and the fruits of skunkberry, hackberry, cedar elm, croton, and a wide variety of other foods in winter.

Turkeys can scratch through snow a foot deep as long as it does not crust over. When snow is on the ground, turkeys also feed on windswept ridges or south-facing slopes where the snow cover is thin. Springs are another favorite winter feeding place. Depending on the source and temperature of the ground water, some springs may remain open even when air temperatures are well below zero Fahrenheit. Turkeys find snails, fern fronds, grasses, sedges, mast, crayfishes, salamanders, snails, earthworms, aquatic insects, and seeds along these spring runs. D. T. Walls found that some springs in Pennsylvania contained an average of three grams of turkey food per square foot.

Turkeys find in tree buds another source of winter food and, like ruffed grouse, they are occasionally seen "budding" (eating tree buds and/or blooms) in beech (Wheeler) and hop hornbeam trees. The buds of beech and hop hornbeam accounted for 21 percent of the winter diet of turkeys in Pennsylvania (Hayden, 1969), but the birds also feed in ash, hackberry, pin oak, and birch trees.

Wild turkeys are adapted to eating buds and other small browse (catkins and pine needles) on which quail, partridges, and pheasants would soon starve, but they are not so efficient in feeding upon them as grouse. In Wisconsin (Dreis *et al.*), turkeys even peeled the bark from jack pine trees and ate the inner cellulose layer. A. Starker Leopold (1953) studied the intestinal structure of turkeys, grouse, bobwhite quail, partridges, and pheasants, and found that both grouse and turkeys have larger intestines and caeca (blind pouches leading off the intestine) in proportion to their body size than pheasants, quail, or partridges. The larger intestinal tract permits turkeys and grouse to digest relatively poor bulk foods more efficiently. It also offers more storage room for breakdown of carbohydrates by microorganisms and provides more absorptive area in the intestinal wall. Thus turkeys are structurally adapted to use low-quality foods during periods of winter stress.

The most threatening weather for turkeys is a severe ice storm followed by long periods of cold and continued ice cover. Turkeys may die of exposure if they become wet before temperatures drop and then the rain begins to freeze. A prolonged ice cover will also prevent the survivors from eating buds and seeds that are normally available above the snow. Turkeys can endure a week or more of severe winter weather without food (Gerstell), but if ice persists longer some will die from starvation. Ordinarily, turkeys may lose one third of their normal body weight without permanent injury (Mosby and Handley, Hayden and Nelson). Nevertheless, there is individual variation in this ability to survive; some turkeys have died after losing 20 percent of their weight while others survived after losing 47 percent (Gardner and Arner).

In severe winter weather, turkeys may remain on the roost for long periods without feeding. For example, the superintendent of Pennsylvania's Wild Turkey Farm reported that during a winter storm turkeys remained on the roost for eight days until the weather moderated. During this time 30 inches of snow fell. Food was available below the roost, but the birds would not fly down to it.

The daily movements of turkeys diminish as the snow becomes deeper and the weather more severe. In Michigan, during periods of deep snow, turkeys moved about within 2 to 160 acres each day. The home range used throughout the winter averaged 683 acres for eight flocks of gobblers, 435 acres for seven flocks of hens, and 492 acres for six flocks containing both sexes.

Prolonged deep snow and low temperatures can eventually cause deaths from starvation among wild turkeys. Substantial losses were reported a number of times during the eighteenth and nineteenth centuries (Schorger, 1966). In recent times the largest loss was that reported in 1968–69 by biologists in Wisconsin. In a five-day period, 35 inches of snow fell. For thirty days the temperature never rose above 15 degrees Fahrenheit and remained below zero, twenty-five of the thirty days. On January 2 they found carcasses of twelve starved turkeys. By January 15 the ground was covered with a fluffy snow 34 inches deep. When deep fluffy snow covers the ground, turkeys will avoid walking in it and may fly from the roost to the feeding area. This time, however, the turkeys refused to walk or fly; they sat in the trees and starved. Predation on the weakened birds became severe, and in spring biologists could account for only slightly more than 100 of the estimated 1,200 turkeys that began the winter (Dreis *et al.*).

Turkeys in the South seldom experience winter periods of prolonged low temperatures, deep snow, or food shortage. In southern hardwood forests, several foods are common among litter on the forest floor. James Kennamer and Dale Arner found an average of 135 pounds of food per acre in such an area. Sugarberry and grape seeds were

96

the most abundant items. Pecans, grape seeds, and green matter were preferred by the turkeys. A longleaf pine forest provided only 10.3 pounds of food per acre (Parker)—one reason why pine forests are generally less attractive to turkeys.

By late winter all turkeys are adult size, and only the larger predators are a threat. Raccoons and bobcats have been credited with killing roosting turkeys at night, but the horned owl is the most effective night predator. A turkey roosting on a limb without overhead branches for protection is in a precarious position. The horned owl weighs three to four pounds and, considering its speed, represents a substantial missile hurtling through the air to bury its talons deep in the turkey's back. The owl strikes the turkey near its wing bases and generally leaves characteristic talon marks in the neck. It plucks feathers from its avian prey before eating, then begins feeding on the head and eats rearward. Such characteristics of predation by horned owls, and by other predators, permit the biologist to determine which one fed upon the turkey and also whether or not it probably killed it, since predators will feed on carrion, or dead turkeys, just as readily as upon those they might kill.

Eagles have been observed preying on Merriam's, Rio Grande, and

The horned owl preys on roosting turkeys (Tennessee Game and Fish Commission).

Eastern turkeys in winter. Of the two eagles, the golden seems to be the more frequent predator, although the bald eagle is also known to prey on wild turkeys (C. Smith and D. Holbrook, personal communications).

Several persons have given basically similar accounts of hunting behavior by pairs of golden eagles (Schorger, 1966; Thomas *et al.,* 1964*b*). When the turkeys see the eagles, they run under trees or brush to escape. One of the eagles alights and walks toward the turkeys, driving them into the open; the other eagle then swoops down and attacks. Savage as it may seem, predation is and always will be a natural part of the turkey's ecology, and history has proved again and again that only man, through his influence on turkey habitats, holds the key to the continuing presence and abundance of this fine game bird.

The golden eagle is another predator (U.S. Fish and Wildlife Service).

Man and Turkey

Turkeys have always been of more than idle curiosity to man. For at least 1,500 years they have provided him with food and adornments. W. A. Ritchie reported that awls, beads, and spoons made from turkey bones were found in archaeological diggings in New York State. In the eastern United States, Indians wove turkey feathers into garments. Turkey spurs were used for arrow points, and quills from the large wing feathers were used to fletch the shafts of arrows.

Indians domesticated turkeys in Mexico, the southwestern United States, North Carolina, and Virginia, some as early as A.D. 400 (Olsen). Many of the Indian tribes of the eastern United States did not domesticate turkeys, however; they were so abundant and easy to kill that it was unnecessary to raise these birds. At a refuse pile near an Indian camp in Kentucky, W. S. Webb reported that turkey bones were exceeded in number only by those of deer, and turkeys have been one of the more abundant food remains found in similar middens throughout the eastern United States. Other Indian tribes had religious or superstitious customs which forbade the eating of certain wild animals; for example, wild turkeys, doves, and quail were taboo food items for the Apaches (Castetter and Opler).

The Pueblo Indians domesticated turkeys to a greater extent than any other tribe. Between A.D. 475 and 700, they made blankets of turkey-feather cord, using both the small downy feathers and heavier

99

feathers from which the stiffer part of the quill had been removed. H. M. Wormington believed that the Pueblos could not have eaten these turkeys, because their bones have not been found in Pueblo food refuse piles but at burial sites with corn and other mortuary offerings.

Spanish explorers wrote of turkeys which they found good eating but which the Indians kept only for their feathers. When Cortez and his men entered the Valley of Mexico in 1519, they found that Montezuma had a large menagerie of hawks, owls, and eagles that were fed about 500 domesticated turkeys daily (Schorger, 1966). The Spaniards took home the Mexican wild turkey, the race domesticated by the Aztecs, and by the early 1600s it had spread throughout Europe. Colonists later brought these turkeys back to America.

As a result, our present domesticated turkeys are descended from the Mexican subspecies, which differs in several ways (described in the first chapter) from the Eastern wild turkey native to the eastern United States. (Of the seven main varieties of today's domestic turkeys, the largest is the bronze, which is most like our wild turkey in coloration; bronze males weigh up to 36 pounds, hens to 16 pounds. The other varieties are slightly smaller and may be white, reddish, brown, slate, or black.) Poultry experts have bred them to develop larger breasts and thighs and shorter legs and necks, so that the Pilgrims would be surprised to see the size of our largest domestic turkeys today.

Early explorers wrote in their journals about wild turkeys in the eastern forests. G. Alsop reported seeing hundreds in the woods of Maryland in the 1880s, and great flocks sometimes passed the doors of the colonists in eastern Massachusetts. During the seventeenth century in southwestern Maine one could see sixty broods of young turkeys sunning themselves in a single morning (Josselyn). Flocks of up to 500 birds were seen leaving their roosts at sunrise in the swamps of North Carolina (Lawson). In Kentucky in 1775 wild turkeys were so abundant that they looked like one continuous flock scattered everywhere in the

In the 1800s, wild turkeys were still abundant in the Southwest (Texas Parks and Wildlife Department).

woods. In parts of Ohio there were sometimes as many as 5,000 turkeys in a flock (Smyth). Two men in Scotland County, Missouri, carried their guns with them one day while husking corn and killed 132 turkeys. At one of the so-called circle hunts in Licking County, Ohio, in 1817, a five-square-mile area was enclosed and 350 turkeys were found within it. This number represents the equivalent of a population density of one turkey per nine acres—almost double the highest population densities known today in the United States (one turkey per sixteen acres along the Mississippi River).

The Texas–Oklahoma area apparently had some of the greatest concentrations of turkeys. There is a report of 10,000 in one drove south of Lawton, Oklahoma (Griswold). Hunters saw flocks containing 3,000 turkeys as late as 1877 near Crawford, Oklahoma (Lane). A thousand turkeys occupied a roost near a camp at Kingfisher, Oklahoma (Knott). In two nights hunters filled two army wagons with turkeys near San Antonio, Texas. On the flat areas of the shortgrass prairie, where the only trees grow along river bottoms, large numbers of turkeys were visible for great distances. (Rio Grande turkeys, as we have seen, tend to congregate in larger winter flocks than the other subspecies.) Even in modern times biologists in Texas and Oklahoma have counted 500 wild turkeys in a single winter roosting place.

When wild turkeys were so abundant, they had no fear of man. In some Indian tribes, like the Cherokee, only the children hunted turkeys; the braves saved their energy for wild game considered tastier and more wary. By the time Cherokee children were ten years old, they were expert at killing small animals with a dart blown through a hollow cane. It was necessary to shoot turkeys in the eye; even so, reportedly, the youngsters seldom missed.

Early journals indicate that colonists and settlers also had little difficulty approaching to within easy gunshot range of turkeys. During the seventeenth century the settlers were dependent on wild game as a regular source of meat because their below-subsistence agriculture made other food sources essential. (They also used the primary feathers to make writing quills.) As long as they shot only what they could use, the large flocks of turkeys were diminished only slightly, becoming scarce only near settlements. During this period wild turkeys were generally plentiful, and there was no commercial market for them. By the beginning of the nineteenth century, however, as towns and cities grew larger, deer, wild turkeys, and wild ducks became common in markets of the Atlantic coast, where they were shipped by wagonload or train carload. Turkeys sold for 6 cents each, sometimes up to 25 cents for one weighing 25 to 30 pounds (Judd); by 1900, wild turkeys had grown so much scarcer that a large one brought $5 on the Chicago market.

As turkeys grew more scarce and more expensive, it became profitable for men to hunt in areas where only small flocks remained. The result was predictable. Wild turkeys were common in Bay City, Michigan, about 1880, for example (Cook), but within fifteen years they had been eliminated from the state.

Although market hunting and trapping were the last stages in their near extinction, they have not been the most destructive factors for wild turkey populations. Land clearing for agriculture, harvesting timber, and uncontrolled fires were even more devastating. Though large flocks of turkeys remained in the Midwest and South at the beginning of the nineteenth century, they had already vanished in parts of the Atlantic Seaboard which had been more thoroughly developed by man. Destroying habitat—the place where an animal lives—is the most effective way to eliminate the animal. Turkeys were gone from Connecticut by 1813 (Zimmer), Vermont by 1842, Massachusetts by 1851 (Bent), Minnesota by 1871 (A. Leopold), Ohio by 1903, Nebraska by 1915 (Zimmer), and South Dakota by 1920. In Missouri the original range included the entire state, but by 1910 turkeys existed only in the Ozarks and the southeastern lowlands (J. B. Lewis, 1967). In many other states turkeys survived only in the more isolated mountains or

Forest destruction effectively eliminates wild turkeys (U.S. Forest Service).

in large forested places along rivers.

In Kentucky, turkey hunting was an important sport as late as the early 1900s (Hardy, 1960). The birds were first protected there after the 1915 hunting season. The turkey population reached its lowest point in that state by 1945, when the only survivors were within the Kentucky Woodlands National Wildlife Refuge.

Declines in the wild turkey population came later in the western states. The Merriam's turkey reached its low point in 1942 (Ligon). By 1920, wild turkeys were gone from their ancestral range in eighteen of the thirty-eight states in which they were originally found and from Ontario. By 1941 the wild turkey occupied not more than 28 percent of its former North American range (Mosby and Handley).

Then began the years of restoring the birds in many states from which they had been eliminated—Michigan, Indiana, Ohio, New York, Massachusetts, Vermont, and others. A few wild turkeys were also established in California, Montana, Oregon, and other states where they had never been seen before. But in many states where wild turkeys originally existed, the present occupied range is still only a small fraction of that occupied when the first settlers came. This is especially true in the Midwest and Northeast. Suitable habitat is no longer available to support turkeys in many of these areas.

The turkey was once so much a part of America that it was considered for our national emblem, instead of the bald eagle; Benjamin Franklin was one of its leading proponents (Wright, page 337). But no longer is the wild turkey an element of everyday life. It is rare to hear expressions like "talk turkey" or "proud as a turkey." In states from which turkeys have been gone for a hundred years, only the names of topographic features—Turkey Mountain, Gobbler Ridge—remind us that turkeys were once native there. Turkey shoots are still held in many parts of the eastern United States, but the actual shooting is at a paper target, and the turkey prize is usually a paunchy domestic bird already cleaned, plucked, and wrapped in glistening plastic. But of course turkeys are still symbolic of fall and the Thanksgiving holiday, with the turkey-raising industry grossing more than $350 million a year and producing over 80 million birds.

Wild turkeys seem to require solitude, in the sense of freedom from repeated disturbance by man. The amount of interference they will

"Proud as a turkey" (U.S. Fish and Wildlife Service).

tolerate seems to vary with the purity of their bloodlines; pen-reared or hybrid birds seem to adjust better to the frequent presence of man. Horace Gore found that turkey populations in Texas declined in direct proportion to human occupation of the land.

Disturbance by man causing hens to abandon their nests has been reported in a number of studies. Henry Mosby and Charles Handley reported that 30 percent of the nests they found were deserted. Robert Wheeler observed five nests, all of which were eventually abandoned, although it required two or three visits before three of the hens deserted. J. S. Ligon reported 16 percent of twelve turkey nests lost through desertion. Of course the activities of the observer magnify the chances for desertion; as a result, figures from this type of study would not apply to all nesting turkeys in a specific area. Certainly some nests are deserted as a result of spring hunting, but it is doubtful if the true percentage is enough to limit turkey populations, as some opponents of spring hunting have implied. Hens that leave the nest will renest elsewhere, as will those hens whose nests are broken up by predators. Because nests are generally well situated to take advantage of surrounding plants and camouflaging plumage patterns, hens will stay on their nests until the last possible moment; hunters can pass within a few feet of a nest and hen without being aware of their presence.

Poaching is another way man threatens turkeys; the actual proportion of the wild turkey population removed by poachers varies from an estimated 3 to 10 percent. Poachers include not only the man who pursues wild game at all seasons and by any means but also the hunter who shoots turkeys illegally while legally seeking other forest game and the man hunting turkeys during the proper season who shoots *any* turkey, legal or not, and usually doesn't know the sex of the bird until after he has shot it. A last type of poacher would be the hunter who exceeds the bag limit.

Poaching methods vary from driving along woods roads and shoot-

The protective coloration of a nesting hen (U.S. Forest Service).

ing turkeys from the vehicle, to tracking flocks in snow in winter or roost hunting at night. Baiting birds with grain and shooting them from a blind or shooting frying-sized poults in the fields in August are other kinds of poaching. Roost hunting is especially detrimental; the violators, armed with bright lights, sneak beneath the winter roosts where large numbers of turkeys are easily located on their traditional roost trees and shoot the birds while they are stupefied by the glare. Pole traps, effective devices formerly used by market hunters, are seldom used by today's poachers because they are easily seen and reported by law-abiding persons.

Ready to respond. At the moment the tom gobbles, his head and neck will extend forward (South Dakota Department of Game, Fish and Parks).

The turkey hunt is one of the greatest outdoor sports, but it is no place for the meat hunter, because even the best shot may not be successful every year, especially if he is a purist who refuses to bush-whack a turkey and shoots only the old gobbler that comes to his call. Whether you carry a gun or a camera, few types of hunting in the United States require as much knowledge of woods lore and animal behavior as locating a turkey gobbler and then successfully calling him to you, and for those who have experienced it, the spring turkey hunt is the favorite.

The first step is to scout the woods before the season opens. Turkeys favor certain areas and will use them for many years if they remain unchanged. Look for tracks along a woods road, feathers by a dust bath, or droppings beneath a roost.

The best time to locate the tom turkey in spring is from thirty minutes or more before sunrise to two hours afterward. At that time he will gobble frequently for the first hour or so. (Later in the season he may gobble for two or three hours or longer.) Most hunters know that turkeys gobble early, so they quit hunting by 10 or 11 A.M.

If you don't hear a turkey in ten or fifteen minutes, try another location. Or perhaps a tom is in the vicinity but just not gobbling; if so, maybe you can stimulate him to speak up. I imitate the call of the barred owl; some hunters imitate the gobble. Of course, a tom will respond to the hen's call, but I prefer not to do this until I know where the tom is and have selected a place to hide in and call from.

Deciding exactly where the gobbler is can be difficult. The distance the gobble can be heard and the direction from which the sound seems to come are influenced by topography, wind direction and veloc-ity, the direction in which the tom is facing, and the extent to which the new year's foliage is out. If you try calling from too far away, he will ignore you. When other hunters are nearby, you will want to get fairly close so you can compete with the other callers, but if you mis-judge you may walk too close and frighten him. You should be acquainted with the topography where you are hunting so you will not have a brushy stream bottom or deep ravine between you and the gobbler. You can't afford to wait all morning while he walks around these obstacles.

Selecting a place to hide and to call from is another matter of concern. You can't call a turkey into an area where it is brushy; he will refuse to strut and court in an area too overgrown for safety from predators. Old-timers claim you cannot call a turkey downhill. Look for an area with large trees and a thick overhead canopy which "shades out" brush beneath it. Wild turkeys readily walk into these open places.

Anyone who has hunted or otherwise observed turkeys in their natural habitat cannot fail to be impressed by their amazing eyesight. The birds easily detect the outline of a hunter and can observe the slightest movement, whether of a minute insect an inch from their bill or a gray squirrel two hundred yards away. Old-time turkey hunters went so far as to claim a turkey could detect the human eye looking through a knothole from inside a hollow tree, and many relied on blinds to put them on an equal footing. Any movement by the hunter must be slight and slow. Even the most amorous strutting gobbler quickly loses his interest in a hen turkey when he sees something suspicious. His neck stretches and stiffens and his head turns sideways (to permit better focusing with one eye). Then is the time to shoot, for your bird can disappear in a wink—and probably will.

Often a hunter does not have time to build a blind. (An exception would be the hunter who knows where the tom courts or roosts and builds a blind there in advance.) He must then take advantage of all natural hiding spots that are available—a large log or a depression left by the roots of a wind-blown tree, any spot where he is well concealed but can have freedom of movement.

There are a wide variety of calls and calling methods, but the hen's yelp is imitated most frequently. Some hunters scorn elaborate mechanical aids and rely only on a leaf of the proper size and texture. (One hunter in Tennessee who forgot his call brought in a gobbler that he had coaxed close enough for a shot by clucking on his pipe-stem.) A very few hunters can cluck and yelp using only their vocal chords.

The most common turkey caller is the box call, which has many commercial and homemade variations; one is a hollowed-out block of cedar with a hinged top that can be swung back and forth. These are good yelpers (in dry weather) and can be modified to make "gobble boxes," used to locate and call up an infuriated tom that is ready to deal with a competitor for his hen.

The slate call requires a flat piece of thin slate and a corncob with a cedar stick or nail in its end. (Another type uses one end of a coconut shell with a cedar or laurel stick protruding outward from the center.) To imitate the yelp or *keouk* sound, the hunter rubs the end of the stick across the slate. Both the slate and the box call make high-pitched yelps.

A variety of calls are used to attract the gobbler (Ted Borg, South Carolina Wildlife Resources Department).

The wing-bone call uses a hen turkey's radius, the smaller of the two bones in the second joint of the wing. (It is usually taken from a small domestic hen turkey, because the wild hen is seldom available and the gobbler's bone is larger and gives a less desirable tone.) It is made by cutting off the ends of the bone, which exposes air spaces in the center, and inserting the small wing bone into the end of a larger bone to amplify the sound. The caller then sucks sharply on the smaller bone to imitate the cluck.

The snuff can, my favorite call, gives a deeper tone. It is made from a Garrett's Scottish Sweet Snuff can, or a can of similar size, 1¾ inches high and 1 inch in diameter. First, punch a hole in the bottom of the can. Next, cut away half the lid but leave the side rim intact. Then stretch surgical rubber over half the open end of the can and replace the lid so that the intact part of the lid almost meets the free edge of the rubber. To call, place your upper lip around the *outer* edge of the rim and your lower lip along the free edge of the rubber. Blow lightly. The breaking sound of each yelp is made by pulling the lower lip slightly away from the edge of the rubber.

The mouth diaphragm, available commercially, is a small piece of lead forming a half circle an inch across with rubber or plastic stretched within it. It is placed in the upper roof of the mouth and positioned with the tongue; then the caller blows out lightly. This is the most versatile call; with it, the expert can imitate any call a turkey can make and still have both hands free.

Some hunters insist that calling as little as possible is best. At least that way there is less chance of spooking your bird with an unorthodox sound. I prefer to go by the reaction of the gobbler. I seldom call as often as he gobbles, unless he is slow in responding. If he is eager and gobbles frequently (several times a minute), I answer every second or third gobble. If he stays out where I first heard him and calls every five to fifteen minutes, I answer most gobbles and try to add enough clucks and trills to intrigue him.

111

One of the most thrilling and exasperating birds to pursue is the wise old tom that stays a hundred yards or so from you and is reluctant to approach closer. Some hunters team up to hunt such birds; if one hunter positions himself sixty to a hundred yards in front of the hunter doing the calling, he will usually get a shot at the gobbler as the bird circles the area from which the sound of the call is coming.

Commercial records that imitate hens or entire flocks of mating turkeys are legal in some states, but for most hunters this only adds artificiality to an otherwise pleasant sport.

I do not use camouflage clothing for hunting, but it can be helpful. Many states require that some bright apparel be worn as a safety precaution; sometimes this law is not enforced for turkey hunting. Some hunters use dark makeup to hide the glare of their faces, which are conspicuous against a background of forest colors. Camouflage netting over the face also discourages mosquitoes and deer flies. Some hunters carry a small collapsible canvas blind with them and cut greenery to place alongside to add to its appearance of authenticity. You must be well hidden if you expect to call the turkey in close.

The most popular shotgun for turkey hunting is the 12-gauge. I like No. 4 shot, but many use No. 6. A double-barreled gun or pump provides added assurance that a crippled bird won't escape. Rifles are used by some hunters in the East but are more useful in the West for hunting the Rio Grande turkey on the prairie or the Merriam's turkey in mature forests of ponderosa pine. All hunters should be familiar with their gun's pattern and range before they hunt.

Muzzle loaders and archery equipment give the turkey a more sporting chance. Along with the other skills required for success, hunters who use these weapons require additional talents: generally they must call the turkey closer and shoot with greater accuracy. Care in choosing weapons and in shooting will ensure that fewer turkeys are crippled and escape to die elsewhere. Crippling losses have been reported to involve 3 percent (Mosby and Handley) to 12 percent (Kozicky) of the

A successful hunt (Wisconsin Conservation Department).

total population, with one bird crippled for every three or four
bagged.

Most of the foregoing comments are also true for the fall hunt. The
area is scouted in advance in the same way, but there is no need
to rise before daybreak, since the turkeys will be moving most of the
day and hunters may stay out as long as they wish. It is unlikely that
gobbling will be heard, because the turkeys will be in their brood
flocks. Some hunters, using a small dog to trail these flocks, rush in
among the birds and scatter them. Then they quickly build a blind
in the vicinity and call to the scattered birds. Since they are anxious
to rejoin their brood mates, the turkeys will usually respond.

Turkeys may be bushwhacked by the still hunter (the hunter who
sits and waits for game) if he becomes familiar with their feeding
behavior. To do this he builds his blind near a field border, along

a woods road, or in a small wooded valley that turkeys use frequently. This type of hunting requires both patience and a knowledge of turkey behavior.

Stalking, another form of turkey hunting, also requires patience, stealth, sharp eyesight, and a knowledge of the habitat frequented by turkeys. The stalker cannot hope to approach a sharp-eyed turkey in the open forest. He uses brush or hilly topography to hide his movements. Every few hundred yards he steps up to the hilltop and looks carefully down the opposite slope. In flat bottomland forest he uses brushy areas to screen his walking, periodically moving to the edge to scan a new area where a turkey may be feeding. In northern states it is sometimes possible to track turkeys in the snow during late fall; in such circumstances it is possible to combine tracking and stalking. Binoculars are useful for locating feeding birds. Slow, stealthy movements will improve the chances for success. The stalking hunter must be alert for others; he risks the ire of the still hunter and the caller whenever he walks up to their position.

For me, the pleasure of turkey hunting diminishes in direct proportion to the number of other hunters I see, especially if they are discourteous and unsportsmanlike. Nothing spoils a hunt faster than having another hunter, hoping to benefit from your efforts, intentionally move between you and the gobbler you are calling. On the other hand, I do not resent that hunter who is calling and competing fairly for the same gobbler as I.

Safety should be the keynote of every hunt. A hunter must never shoot until certain of the identity of his quarry. Even experts can be fooled by a hunter imitating a wild turkey's call. (I have also heard a few squeaky-voiced hens that I thought were hunters doing a poor job of imitation.) Occasionally two hunters will be calling each other, each believing the other to be a turkey. Therefore, blind shots in the direction of supposed turkey sounds are unforgivable.

Hunters should eviscerate their birds soon after shooting, unless the weather is very cold. Proper field dressing is the first step toward ensuring that a wild bird will taste well when cooked. Once home, the hunter can still determine the live weight fairly accurately by increasing the dressed weight 12 to 13 percent. The fully cleaned bird (with feathers, head, and lower legs removed) will weigh about three fourths of its live weight.

Where hunting is for gobblers only, about 5 to 8 percent of the total turkey population is harvested. When fall hunting of either sex is legal, an average of 30 percent of the population is taken. In some areas where hunting is intensive, the harvest has been as high as 46 percent of the estimated fall population. Thirty-five states now allow turkey hunting in spring and/or fall. The Big Game Inventory figures published by the United States Fish and Wildlife Service indicated a nationwide harvest of 128,167 wild turkeys in 1968.

The primary feathers indicate age differences.

YOUNG   ADULT

A hunter may be interested in knowing how old his turkey is. From the time turkeys hatch until they are more than six months old, it is possible to determine their birth date fairly accurately. The technique relies on measuring the primary feathers, the ten large flight feathers, from the point where they emerge from the skin to their tips, and then checking these measurements on a chart showing the average lengths of the same feathers on birds of known age. To the hunter this is just an added bit of interesting information. For the biologist, it provides a valuable clue to the success of that summer's hatch. Biologists can distinguish a young-of-the-year bird by several other methods, such as examining the bird's vent (anus) to see if a saclike pouch opens into the back surface of the large intestine; the pouch disappears in turkeys more than eight months old (Mosby and Handley).

Several plumage characteristics are also useful for determining the age of a wild turkey. The easiest check for hunters is to examine the outermost primary (wing) feather at the tip. For birds less than twelve to fourteen months old, this feather is generally sharply pointed at its tip and lacks the alternating light and dark bars; in older turkeys it is rounded, and the alternating bars extend to the tip. Also, in a yearling turkey, as we saw, the two center tail feathers are longer than the rest; in the adult, all tail feathers are about the same length and form a perfect fan when spread.

Management

RAIN SPATTERED AGAINST the windshield. Gusts of cool February wind lightly rocked the car. We had been waiting since dawn at the trap site for a flock of Rio Grande turkeys. By 9 A.M. we began to wonder what had gone wrong. Usually at this time the turkeys were feeding here. But many things can interfere with a successful catch: poachers, or maybe even neighboring ranchers, resentful of having "their" turkeys trapped and removed, even though the flocks are on their property only because of past restocking programs. (Fortunately there are generally some landowners who will permit state conservation agencies to trap on their property.)

We were in western Oklahoma with a drop-net trap and using a car as a blind, about 150 yards from the trap. I remembered blinds I had used in Tennessee and Michigan—well-camouflaged, small, cold, cramped structures of canvas or burlap over a light framework. Here we waited in a white station wagon in the middle of a pasture, with the heater running and the radio playing. Some Eastern turkeys would have been frightened by the car, but Rio Grande turkeys are used to seeing farm trucks and machinery across the prairie landscape and are not spooked by a stationary vehicle.

Finally the first birds of a flock of 160 crossed the brow of a hill. They were grazing on the tender green shoots of winter wheat, feeding calmly and walking slowly, but pausing periodically, heads

Turkeys beneath the drop net, before ...
and after (Oklahoma Department of Wildlife Conservation).

erect, to look for danger. Several eager individuals ran ahead as they neared the trap site. With a few flaps of their wings they went over the fence separating the wheat field from the pasture where our drop net was stretched, eight feet above the wheat and milo seeds we had spread about for bait.

The turkeys had been eating our bait for a week, but we had set up the net just the previous afternoon. The birds looked carefully and approached cautiously but were not frightened by the large tentlike net as long as it didn't flap. Fortunately the rain had stopped and the air was calm. Twenty, then thirty birds moved under the net. My companion said, "We won't drop the net unless at least forty turkeys are under it. If we don't get that many under the net today, we probably will tomorrow." (In Tennessee we had been happy when half a dozen Eastern wild turkeys entered our bait site.)

It looked as though we wouldn't drop the net that day. Then, at last, one large group of turkeys moved to the bait, so that about sixty were now feeding there. We probably had as many birds on the bait as we would get that day. "Now?" I asked, looking at my companion. He nodded in agreement and released the net. Down it came on a surging, leaping mass of turkeys. Here and there a few ran from beneath the net as we rushed to secure the edges. The rest of the flock had flown out of sight. The excitement was over.

Securely entangled in the net, forty-seven captured turkeys leaped and struggled. For two hours we weighed, measured, and banded them and placed them in boxes. The temperature had been dropping, and our fingers were numb. We still had to clean the net and load it for use at another site, but that could wait. Now we had to haul our turkeys to their new home—suitable habitat that had been unoccupied for fifty years. On the way we drank hot coffee and talked about other days like this when everything went right and we made a good catch.

One of the most useful developments for the wildlife manager is

A prize catch (Oklahoma Department of Wildlife Conservation).

the modern equipment for capturing wild turkeys. This includes the drop net, the rocket net, and drugged baits. Regardless of the technique used, most turkey trapping is done during the winter when turkeys accept bait readily and the hunting season is over. (Trapping of broods in late summer proved to be a suitable technique in Arkansas, however. According to Gene Rush, summer broods were easier to trap, could be transported with less loss, and would stay in the area where they were released.)

The rocket net fired over a baiting site.

The drop net is used principally for Rio Grande and Merriam's turkeys, where large flocks are common in winter. It is 70 by 70 feet with a 1¾-inch mesh and is suspended on poles six to ten feet above the ground. The area beneath the net is baited with wheat, corn, or milo. The net falls from the poles when small charges are detonated electrically.

The rocket net is commonly used in eastern forested areas. It is a nylon net of 1¾-inch mesh and varies from 30 by 60 to 60 by 100 feet. Depending on its size, three to six rockets, attached to ropes on the leading edge of the net, are required to fire it up and over the turkeys at a 20- to 45-degree angle. The rockets contain black powder charges that are ignited with electric squibs. The wiring from the squibs leads to a blind where the trapper hides. The bait is placed in front of the net, which is folded and carefully camouflaged with leaves or grass. The rear edge of the net is anchored, with shock-absorbing rubber, to stakes or heavy weights. When the turkeys are in proper

Turkeys baited to the pole or drop-door trap (Colorado Game, Fish and Parks Department).

position in front of the net, the trapper discharges the rockets with a battery or plunger-type detonator. Some turkeys occasionally are able to outrun the net, in spite of the high speed of the rockets. A small infolding of the net provides a pocket in which a few birds are caught as they attempt to run from beneath it.

Some western states use a rectangular pole trap, which operates automatically by a trigger tripped by the turkeys and so does not require the presence of an operator. The average catch is much lower than for the drop net, but several traps can be set simultaneously.

Drugged baits have recently been developed as a successful capture technique. (Lovett Williams, of the Florida Game and Freshwater Fish Commission, has done much work in this field, having pioneered in the use of alpha chloralose, the first effective drug used,

122

Releasing the catch by aerial drop in unoccupied habitat (Florida Game and Fresh Water Fish Commission).

and having directed work with other drugs.) The technique requires less investment in equipment, and only one man is needed. The trapper baits an area and, when turkeys start using it, determines how many are accepting bait, so he will know how much will capture the entire flock. Next day he puts out drugged bait and watches from a blind until the birds are in a satisfactory state of narcosis (about fifteen minutes). Then he approaches the birds quietly, sometimes using a net to capture them, weighs them, and places a band on one leg. The birds are confined in large cardboard boxes until they recover from the drug (within ten hours—Williams et al., 1972b). Tribromoethanol is the most satisfactory drug tested to date.

In spite of new techniques, it still requires lots of hard work to

This Florida gobbler is in an early stage of narcosis after eating seeds mixed with alpha chloralose (Lovett Williams).

Turkeys readily accept bait in northern states when snow is on the ground
(Michigan Department of Natural Resources).

trap turkeys. Sometimes you wait in the blind only a few hours before they come to the bait; at other times it takes several days. Trapping is a dawn-to-dusk job when the trapper is prebaiting several spots, waiting for birds at one trap site, locating other flocks where baiting can begin, carrying, setting, and camouflaging traps, and transporting captured birds to a new release site.

Attempts to restore turkeys began in the late 1940s. Most states already had game-bird farm facilities which could be used to rear turkeys, and brood stock was generally available from pen-reared birds that included some wild blood. Some game departments attempted to maintain the wild characteristics by the back-crossing method, whereby three-fourths-wild hens were wing-clipped and

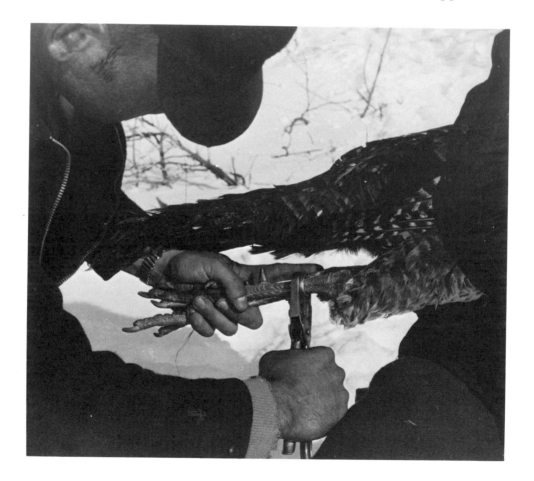

Wild-trapped turkeys are banded prior to release (John Hall, Vermont Fish and Game).

placed in large isolated enclosures where wild gobblers could fly in and out at will to mate with them, producing young with predominantly wild genetic characteristics. Unfortunately, rearing birds in captivity favors survival of the tamest birds; the wilder ones are more apt to injure themselves by flying against the fence at every approach of the caretaker. Repeated back-crossing with wild stock was the only way any wild characteristics could be maintained in the brood stock.

While thousands of pen-reared turkeys were released, wild populations were successfully re-established in only a few cases. Pen-reared birds are simply not sufficiently adapted for survival in the wild. A. S. Leopold (1944) named some of the reasons: (1) hybrid hens nest earlier, (2) they select more open and unprotected spots for their nests, and (3) the poults are more susceptible to predators and to death by exposure. Pen-reared birds also find it difficult to learn to feed on native wild foods while avoiding man and other predators. Some react by heading for the nearest farmyard where they can find the handouts they are accustomed to. There they become further domiciled or contract poultry diseases which decimate their ranks. In some places where pen-reared turkeys were released to bolster small wild populations, the releases may have been more detrimental than beneficial, since the released birds introduced diseases into the wild populations. Thus, the first attempts to re-establish turkeys in parts of their original range failed.

The development of effective capture techniques is what made subsequent restoration programs successful, since it became possible to trap enough wild turkeys to restock much of the suitable habitat where turkeys had been eliminated. (Twelve to fifteen wild turkeys, including two to three gobblers, are sufficient to start a new population.) By this kind of management, wildlife biologists have increased turkey populations until today they can be seen and enjoyed by many persons throughout the country. Henry Mosby estimated that there were 1.25 million wild turkeys in the United States in 1970, based on a compilation of each state's census work.

Census is essential to proper management of any wild animal. When a decreasing population flashes a warning that something is wrong, the biologist must determine where the problem is and how to correct it. Population estimates are like a pulse rate. From the information received, the biologist can judge what proportion of the population can be harvested, and the hunting season length and bag limits can be set accordingly.

Turkeys are counted in several ways. One method is based on gobbling routes, which extend 15 to 30 miles through turkey range. In the spring, biologists start their census routes about thirty minutes before sunrise and continue for several hours. One technique is to stop for three to five minutes at one-mile intervals along a road and record the number of individual gobblers heard along the route. This census, if compared with counts of previous years, will indicate relative trends in population size. The accuracy of these counts increases with the number of times each route is run and the number of routes in each area.

Another technique has been found useful in western Texas in recent years (R. Cook): the traditional winter roosts are visited and the turkeys are counted as they go to roost.

A third method relies on the cooperation of those persons who frequently see wild turkeys, such as hunters and foresters. Records kept by these people—date, time, location, number, sex, and age of birds—are assembled by the biologist, who then plots the separate flocks on a map. Duplicate counting of the same flock is avoided by noting the distinctive sex, age, and size composition of each group, since each flock retains its identity during a particular season. The total number of birds observed is used to estimate the total population. The accuracy of this type of count depends on the probability that each flock will be seen and recorded. Thus the total population estimate is usually conservative, especially in more inaccessible forest

Dropping of the hen.

Droppings of the gobbler.

areas where good census coverage is not possible.

In northern and western states a snow cover permits a track count, and modern snowmobiles make most areas accessible.

A fifth method, that of an aerial census from helicopters, is currently being tested in the open habitat of the Rio Grande turkey.

Various field signs can tell the observer much about wary turkeys

129

Wild turkey tracks bordering a stream.

that have not been seen. Turkey droppings, molted feathers, and tracks all give clues to the bird's sex. For the Eastern wild turkey (and probably for other subspecies), the dropping size and configuration can be used (Bailey, 1956). Droppings of the adult gobbler may be as much as 15 mm. in diameter; yearling gobblers up to 10 mm.; hens 5 to 8 mm. The hen's dropping is looped, spiral, or bulbous in shape, in contrast to the longer and relatively straight male dropping, which has a knoblike twist at the end. The pancake-shaped caecal dropping is found in all months and is characteristic of both sexes.

Feathers are often found around roosts and dusting or feeding areas. The body feathers show the sex differences already mentioned: the tip of the gobbler feather is black and the hen's fulvous brown or white.

Tracks are a third field sign that is helpful to naturalists and hunters. Sandy loam soils, mud, or wet snow are bases for distinct tracks. The mature gobbler's track measurements and length of stride are characteristic. Lovett Williams (1959) determined that the adult Eastern gobbler's stride measured between 11.9 and 14.2 inches and the hen's between 7.3 and 10.9 inches. A straight line drawn between the tips of the outer toes will usually intersect pad number one of the middle toe in gobblers and pad number two in hens. A track with a spread over 4.75 inches and a mid-toe width greater than 0.5 inch will probably be a gobbler's. Also, for Eastern wild turkeys, when the measurement from the middle toe claw to the back of the heel pad is more than 4.25 inches, the turkey making the track is a gobbler (Mosby and Handley). Occasionally some type of foot deformity will permit identification of an individual bird. In spring one may find lines paralleling both sides of a turkey's tracks for a distance of several feet. These are the marks of wing tips dragged on the ground when the gobbler struts.

In addition to restocking and census programs, turkeys are also managed by modifying their habitat. Surface water is an important part of turkey range; therefore, some wildlife managers try to develop a water hole within every square mile of public land managed for wildlife. Hens seem to build their nests within a quarter mile of water. Turkeys readily use mud puddles, small ponds, lakes, or rivers for drinking. There is, however, no record of turkeys bathing in shallow water, as smaller birds do.

Fields can be managed for the turkeys' benefit by planting small areas in agricultural crops. To biologists these are "food plots," and they range in size from one-quarter acre to several acres. In South Carolina, ladino clover, white Dutch clover, crimson clover, Kentucky 31 fescue, rescue grass, ryegrass, oats, and wheat were com-

Small ponds are an important part of turkey habitat.

pared in pounds of forage and insect protein produced. The three clovers produced more forage at a much lower cost (L. G. Webb, 1963) and contained insect populations two to four times greater; leafhoppers and aphids were especially abundant. (Perennial ryegrass was the most important in the production of beetles, grasshoppers, wasps, and ants.) Clovers have the added advantage of not requiring annual reseeding.

Since fields are so important, it is understandable that cattle, goats, and sheep can be either beneficial or injurious to turkey habitat. Moderate grazing is beneficial; it keeps openings from reverting to forest and prevents the weeds and grasses from becoming so rank that young poults cannot travel through them. On the other hand, overgrazed openings offer turkeys neither food variety nor abundance. Livestock can eliminate turkeys much more effectively through overgrazing than can the hunter or wild predator.

Federal land-clearing programs, particularly in the Southwest, also mean fewer wild turkeys. These programs involve spraying or bulldozing scrub-oak forest or removing mesquite and other shrubs and converting the cleared lands to Bermuda grass or prairie pasture for more cattle. But turkeys do not use the centers of large fields. They stay near the edges where they can escape to brush or timber if the golden eagle or other danger appears. When the brush and trees go, so will the turkeys.

One threat to wild turkeys that has been building for the past three decades is the potential loss from insecticides. Forest lands have not been subject to as much spraying as agricultural areas, but no part of this planet is free from the contamination of insecticides. Only about half of an aerial spray released at treetop level reaches the target area (Graham); the rest is dispersed by wind and water. Turkeys in many areas also rely on agricultural crops for 6 to 10 percent of their annual diet (Korschgen, 1967), and some of these crops are regularly sprayed. Many chemical insecticides, especially the chlorinated hydrocarbons such as DDT, are persistent; that is, they decompose slowly and may remain in the environment for many years, in soil and water. Animals store insecticide (from plants or other animals they consume) in their own tissues, especially in fat cells and some glands. Eventually some upper limit is reached and the animal dies from insecticide poisoning or is left sterile as a result of the insecticide residue. For example, DDT residues inhibit the ability of birds to utilize the calcium stored in their bodies for the production of eggshells.

The resulting thin shells break when the bird tries to incubate its eggs.

The potential exists for losses to turkeys from insecticide poisoning. In some cornfields in Missouri, aldrin has been used as a treatment for corn rootworm control. Korschgen (1970) found that insecticide residues in these fields were capable of killing any young quail that ate twenty of one type of ground beetle. The effect on turkey poults has not been tested, but probably it is equally fatal. In Alabama, reduction of turkey populations followed aerial application of dieldrin and heptachlor (Clawson). Wildlife biologists and conservationists are fighting against the use of persistent insecticides, and DDT has already been banned in a number of states.*

Refuges are no longer considered essential for wild turkey management, although they were once used in a few states to save remaining flocks. As the native population recovered, these refuge flocks provided a source of wild trapped turkeys for restocking, and they have since become management areas where regulated hunting is possible.

Most sportsmen think that the best way to increase game populations is to kill predators (foxes, hawks, owls, and the like). This would be true if predators really limited game populations, but turkey populations are not controlled in this way. The basic limiting factor is the quality of the habitat. If sites for food, water, roosts, brood-rearing, nesting, courting, and other year-round needs are available, turkeys will survive there. Weather, predators, diseases, and parasites will help keep the population stable and within the ability of the habitat to support it. If most of the predators could be removed, which is doubtful, weather, diseases, and parasitism would merely take on a larger share of population regulation.

*On June 13, 1972, William D. Ruckelshaus, Administrator of the Environmental Protection Agency, banned almost all uses of DDT, effective December 31, 1972.—*The Editor.*

Some "wild" turkeys like to get their food the easy way.

Winter feeding, another management measure, is often proposed by sportsmen's groups, the basic premise being that turkeys need supplemental food to survive the winter. Actually the wild turkey is well adapted to survive all but the most extreme winters; it was abundant in pre-colonial times as far north as southern Ontario, without supplemental foods. Under the most severe conditions, some turkeys will die of starvation, but it is doubtful that the starving turkeys would leave the roost even to visit a feeder. Winter feeding programs are also very expensive; for many years, Pennsylvania spent $50,000 to $90,000 annually on winter feeding (Latham, 1959).

In addition, feeding wild turkeys may be detrimental to them, since it favors transmission between them of diseases and parasites, and birds weakened by parasites and diseases are less likely to survive winter weather. Again, feeding programs tend to make the turkeys less self-reliant. If severe weather prevents replenishment of the food, as it sometimes does, the birds are left without food when they need it most. Turkeys that feed regularly at a feeding station are more susceptible to poachers and predators attracted by concentrations of birds. The same birds are also easily attracted to farmyards where they can find easy handouts at other seasons—and thus they become gradually domesticated.

Although winter feeding programs are not necessary over most of the range of the wild turkey, there are some areas where it may be an essential management practice; that is, where the habitat is marginal for turkeys and where winter foods are the limiting factor. Here, sizable flocks can be maintained only through feeding programs.

Controlled burning in the Southeast has been another tool that may benefit turkeys. It is used for timber management, to prepare seed beds, eliminate hardwood undergrowth, and control brown-spot fungus in longleaf pine. Turkeys and quail are helped because favored foods are stimulated to grow in the open areas beneath the pines, and the open understory provides a place where turkeys can see long distances and readily fly or run from predators.

Controlled burning is an important management tool (U.S. Forest Service).

Turkeys Tomorrow

SURVIVAL OF ALL wild animals depends on the whims of men as they alter habitat to fit changing economic patterns and new technology. Certainly the turkey will be no exception. Their populations could diminish drastically in the next century unless people are convinced that they have a value that justifies making an effort to ensure their preservation.

There are still good habitats without turkeys in a number of states which could be stocked. Some of it is in places that have reverted to forest after the former tenants gave up farming and moved off the land. Several western states have such unoccupied range, suitable for Merriam's or Rio Grande turkeys. Eliminating or controlling poaching and more intensive land management for turkeys could bring about a rise in wild turkey populations in many places in the United States.

The wild turkey is basically a bird of the forest, and a practice that will destroy turkeys by eliminating them from woodlands is the increasingly intensive timber management undertaken on both private and public lands to supply our increasing requirements for more and more wood products for housing and paper.

Intensive or high-yield management of tree crops means several things that can be detrimental to turkeys. One is short cutting rotations (the age at which trees are cut), in which trees are felled before

A stately procession. These turkeys were established west of the Rockies, outside their original range (California Department of Fish and Game).

achieving their maximum growth. This means cutting hardwoods for use in paper pulp before they are large enough to provide either wood for lumber or mast for wild turkeys and other animals. Intensive management also may mean the gradual conversion to pine of some stands of hardwoods, such as oaks, beeches, and maples. Pine is a soft wood that grows rapidly in plantations and makes good paper pulpwood and lumber in a relatively short time. Pine plantations are more economical to plant and to harvest because it is possible to use more equipment and less manpower to "crop" them. Pine seeds, however, are of minor food value for turkeys, except for the Merriam's subspecies, and young pine stands are not used by turkeys except for escape from predators and for occasional roosting.

High-yield forestry means maximum yield per unit area. In some bottomland forests we already see detrimental effects on turkeys (Clark). Forest openings—fields or clearings—between stands of timber are unproductive for lumbermen, and trees may be planted in these places which are so important a part of the turkey's habitat. Cottonwoods are very rapid-growing hardwoods that are being planted in plantations and cut in short rotations, perhaps as often as every two years. These provide no foods for turkeys.

Intensive management also requires better control of insect damages to forest land. If this leads to improved biological control of insect pests, it is all to the good. But if insect control means increased chemical spraying of our forests, we should watch for detrimental effects.

The United States Forest Service recognizes that intensive forest management and optimum wildlife management are not always compatible, and they are setting aside areas in some national forests that favor deer, turkeys, or other wild animals, planning to manage these places intensively for the benefit of the particular species being encouraged. Elsewhere, we can expect further loss of game populations as land clearing continues.

At this point, one might suggest that I have overlooked the impact of hunting pressure, but hunting is no problem. The numbers of turkeys that are killed by hunters can be regulated by variations in season lengths and bag limits. One cannot, however, regulate a private owner's management of his land. Our changing land uses, and the economics that affect them, will largely determine the location and the number of turkeys we have in the twenty-first century.

We are as conscious about conservation as any other nation on earth. We hear about ecology every day and are becoming increasingly aware of the complexity and interdependency of animal and plant communities. When we tamper with this system and favor certain members of the community, others are obviously affected. With this realization comes the recognition that careful planning is necessary, before man regulates nature, to assure that this management will be most beneficial for the greatest number.

I only hope that wild turkeys will continue to be sufficiently abundant for everyone to enjoy these birds as so many of us have. The mere desire to see a wild turkey should be enough for most of us to be concerned that there will continue to be tracts of land where one can stalk them, whether armed with binoculars, a camera, or a gun. They are a part of our heritage, one of the last of the truly wild animals of North America.

Scattered clearings are an important part of forest habitat (U.S. Forest Service).

Bibliography

Aldrich, J. W. 1967. Taxonomy, distribution and present status. In *The Wild Turkey and Its Management*. O. H. Hewitt, ed., pp. 17–44. The Wildlife Society, Washington, D.C., 589 pp.

Alsop, G. 1880. *A Character of the Province of Maryland* (1666). Maryland Historical Society Fund, Publication 15.

Anonymous. 1880. *The History of Miami County, Ohio*. Chicago: W. H. Beers and Co.

Bailey, R. W. 1955a. Notes on albinism in the Eastern wild turkey. *Journal of Wildlife Management* 19(3):408.

———. 1955b. Two records of turkey brood survival after death of the hen. *Journal of Wildlife Management* 19(3):408–409.

———. 1956. Sex determination of adult wild turkeys by means of dropping configuration. *Journal of Wildlife Management* 20(2):220.

———. 1964. *Wild Turkey: Population, Trends, Productivity and Harvest*. Annual P-R Project Report, West Virginia Conservation Commission, Charleston, W. Va., 14 pp.

———, and K. T. Rinell. 1967. Events in the turkey year. In *The Wild Turkey and Its Management*, O. H. Hewitt, ed., pp. 73–91. The Wildlife Society, Washington, D.C.

———, and ———. 1968. *History and Management of the Wild Turkey in West Virginia*. West Virginia Department of Natural Resources, Bulletin 6, 59 pp.

Baldwin, S. P., and S. C. Kendeigh. 1938. Variations in the weights of birds. *The Auk* 55(3):416–467.

141

Barwick, L. H., D. H. Austin, and L. E. Williams, Jr. 1970. Roosting of young turkey broods during summer in Florida. *Proceedings of the Annual Conference of the Southeastern Game and Fish Commissioners* 24:231–243.

———, and D. W. Speake. 1972. Seasonal movements and activities of wild turkey gobblers. *Proceedings of the Second National Wild Turkey Symposium,* Columbia, Mo. (at press).

"Basso." 1874. A little turkey story. *Forest and Stream* 2:59.

Beasom, S. L. 1968. Some observations of social hierarchy in the wild turkey. *The Wilson Bulletin* 80(4):489–490.

———. 1970. Productivity of bearded wild turkey hens in south Texas. *Journal of Wildlife Management* 34(1):183–186.

Bent, A. C. 1932. *Life Histories of North American Gallinaceous Birds. Orders Galliformes and Columbiformes.* Smithsonian Institution, U.S. National Museum Bulletin 162, Washington, D.C.

Beyers, L. E. 1939. Rearing wild turkeys in the wild. *Game Breeder and Sportsman* 43(1):2, 3, 14.

Billingsley, B. B., Jr., and D. H. Arner. 1970. The nutritive value and digestibility of some winter foods of the Eastern wild turkey. *Journal of Wildlife Management* 34(1):176–182.

Blakey, H. L. 1937. Wild turkey management on the Missouri Ozark Range. *Transactions of the North American Wildlife and Natural Resources Conference* 2:494–498.

Boeker, E. L., and V. E. Scott. 1969. Roost tree characteristics for Merriam's turkeys. *Journal of Wildlife Management* 33(1):121–124.

Brand, Albert, and P. P. Kellogg. 1939. Auditory responses of starlings, English sparrows, and domestic pigeons. *The Wilson Bulletin* 51(1):38–41.

Burger, G. V. 1954. Wild turkeys in central coastal California. *The Condor* 56(4):198–206.

Burget, M. L. 1957. *The Wild Turkey in Colorado.* Colorado Game and Fish Department, P-R Project W-39-R, 68 pp.

Burroughs, W. T., and T. L. Kosin. 1953. The effects of ambient temperature on production and fertilizing capacity of turkey spermatozoa. *Physiological Zoology* 26:131–146.

Capel, S. W. 1970. *A Nationwide Survey of Turkey Management with Special Emphasis on Hunting Seasons and Regulations.* Wildlife

Bibliography

Bulletin 2, Kansas Forestry, Fish and Game Commission, 26 pp.

Castetter E. F., and M. E. Opler. 1936. Ethnobiological studies in the American southwest. III. The technobiology of the Chiricahua and Mescalero Apache. *University of New Mexico Biological Series* 4(5):1–63.

Clark, H. C. 1972. The present distribution and population density of the wild turkey in Mississippi. *Proceedings of the Second National Wild Turkey Symposium,* Columbia, Mo. (at press).

Clawson, S. G. 1959. A wild turkey population on an area treated with Heptachlor and Dieldrin. *Alabama Birdlife* 6(3–4):4–8.

Clemens, Samuel (Mark Twain). 1906. Hunting the deceitful turkey. *Harper's Magazine* 114:57–58.

Cook, A. J. 1893. *Birds of Michigan.* Michigan Agriculture College Bulletin 94, 168 pp.

Cook, Robert. 1972. A census technique for Rio Grande turkeys in the Edwards Plateau of Texas. *Proceedings of the Second National Wild Turkey Symposium,* Columbia, Mo. (at press).

Cottam, Clarence, C. S. Williams, and C. A. Sooter, 1942. Flight and running speed of birds. *The Wilson Bulletin* 54(2):121–131.

Crockett, B. C. 1969. Quantitative evaluation of winter roosting sites of the Rio Grande turkey in north central Oklahoma. Master of Science thesis, Oklahoma State University, Stillwater, Okla., 45 pp

Dalke, P. D., A. S. Leopold, and D. L. Spencer. 1946. *The Ecology and Management of the Wild Turkey in Missouri.* Technical Bulletin No. 1, Missouri Conservation Commission, 86 pp.

Davis, J. R. 1972. Wild turkey movements in southwest Alabama. *Proceedings of the Second National Wild Turkey Symposium,* Columbia, Mo. (at press).

Davison, V. E. 1962. Taste, not color, draws birds to berries and seeds. *Audubon Magazine* 64(6):346–350.

————, and K. E. Gractz. 1957. Managing habitat for white-tailed deer and wild turkeys. *Transactions of the North American Wildlife and Natural Resources Conference* 22:412–424.

Donohoe, R. W., and C. E. McKibben. 1970. *The Wild Turkey in Ohio.* Ohio Game Monograph No. 3, Ohio Department of Natural Resources, 32 pp.

————, and ————. 1971. *Ohio Turkey Stocking, Distribution, and*

Abundance. Wildlife Inservice Note Number 171, Ohio Department of Natural Resources, Division of Wildlife, 28 pp.

————, ————, and C. B. Lowry. 1968. Turkey nesting behavior. *The Wilson Bulletin* 80(1):103–4.

Dreis, R. E., C. F. Smith, and L. E. Myers. 1972. Wisconsin's turkey experiment. *Proceedings of the Second National Wild Turkey Symposium*. Columbia, Mo. (at press).

Duncan, V. 1945. The snake without a friend. *Southwest Review* 30:167.

Edminster, F. C. 1947. *The Ruffed Grouse*. New York: The Macmillan Company.

Ellis, J. E., and J. B. Lewis. 1967. Mobility and annual range of wild turkeys in Missouri. *Journal of Wildlife Management* 31(3):568–581.

Gardner, D. T., and D. H. Arner. 1968. Food supplements and wild turkey reproduction. *Transactions of the North American Wildlife and Natural Resources Conference* 33:250–258.

Gerstell, R. 1942. *The Place of Winter Feeding in Practical Wildlife Management*. Pennsylvania Game Commission, Research Bulletin 3, 121 pp.

Glover, F. A. 1948. Winter activities of wild turkey in West Virginia. *Journal of Wildlife Management* 12(4):416–427.

Good, H. G., and L. G. Webb. 1940. Spring foods of the wild turkey in Alabama. *American Wildlife* 29(6):288–290.

Gore, Horace. 1972. Land use practices and Rio Grande turkey in Texas. *Proceedings of the Second National Wild Turkey Symposium*, Columbia, Mo. (at press).

Graham, Frank, Jr. 1970. *Since Silent Spring*. Houghton Mifflin Co.

Grigg, G. W. 1957. The structure of stored sperms in the hen and the nature of the release mechanisms. *Poultry Science* 36(2):450–451.

Griswold, Gillett. 1958. Old Fort Sill: the first seven years. *Chronicles of Oklahoma* 36:2–14.

Hale, E. B., and M. W. Schein. 1962. The behavior of turkeys. In *The Behavior of Domestic Animals*. E. S. E. Hafez, ed., Baltimore: The Williams and Wilkins Co.

Hamrick, W. J., and J. R. Davis. 1971. Summer food items of juvenile wild turkeys. *Proceedings of the Annual Conference of the South-*

eastern *Association of Game and Fish Commissioners* 25:85–89.

Hardy, F. C. 1960. Results of stocking wild-trapped and game-farm turkeys in Kentucky. *Proceedings of the First National Wild Turkey Symposium* 1:61–65.

——. 1963. A tradition regained. *Kentucky Happy Hunting Ground* 19(1):2, 30.

Hayden, A. H. 1961. *Winter Range Requirements of the Wild Turkey in Cameron County, Pennsylvania.* Pennsylvania Cooperative Wildlife Research Unit, 7 pp.

——. 1965. Dig those scratching turkey. *Pennsylvania Game News* 36(3):21–23.

——. 1969. Opportunist—yes, picky—no! *Pennsylvania Game News* 40(7):25–29.

——, and E. Nelson. 1963. The effects of starvation and limited rations on reproduction of game-farm wild turkeys. *Proceedings of the Northeastern Wildlife Conference,* Portland, Me.

Henry, V. G. 1969. Predation on dummy nests of ground-nesting birds in the southern Appalachians. *Journal of Wildlife Management* 33(1):169–172.

Hillestad, H. O. 1970. Movements, behavior, and nesting ecology of the wild turkey in east central Alabama. Master of Science thesis, Auburn University, Auburn, Ala., 70 pp.

——. 1972. A telemetric study of the movement and nesting ecology of the Eastern wild turkey in Alabama. *Proceedings of the Second National Wild Turkey Symposium,* Columbia, Mo. (at press).

Hoffman, D. M. 1962. *The Wild Turkey in Eastern Colorado.* Colorado Game and Fish Department, Technical Bulletin No. 12, 47 pp.

——. 1968. Roosting sites and habits of Merriam's turkeys in Colorado. *Journal of Wildlife Management* 32(4):859–866.

Hohn, O. 1961. Endocrine glands, thymus and pineal body. In *Biology and Comparative Physiology of Birds.* A. J. Marshall, ed., pp. 97–115. New York: Academic Press.

Holbrook, H. L. 1972. Wild turkey management in southern forest types. *Proceedings of the Second National Wild Turkey Symposium,* Columbia, Mo. (at press).

Jackson, E. 1942. Handle with care. *Arizona Highways* 18(2):42.

Johnson, R. R. 1961. Aerial pursuit of hawks by turkeys. *The Auk* 78:646.

Jonas, R. J. 1964. Ecology and management of Merriam's turkey in the long pines, southeastern Montana. Ph.D. dissertation, Montana State College, Bozeman, Mont., 118 pp.

————. 1966. *Merriam's Turkeys in Southeastern Montana.* Technical Bulletin 3, Montana Fish and Game Department, 36 pp.

Josselyn, J. 1860. *New England's Rarities Discovered* (1672). Worcester, Mass.: n.p.

Judd, S. D. 1905. *The Grouse and Wild Turkeys of the United States, and Their Economic Value.* United States Department of Agriculture, Bureau of Biological Survey, Bulletin 24, Washington, D.C., 55 pp.

Kanoy, W. C. 1936. How fast can a wild turkey fly? *Field and Stream* 49(11):86–87.

Kellogg, F. E., and V. M. Reid. 1970. Bobwhites as possible reservoir hosts for blackhead in wild turkeys. *Journal of Wildlife Management* 34(1):155–159.

Kendeigh, S. C. 1945. Resistance to hunger in birds. *Journal of Wildlife Management* 9:217–226.

Kennamer, J. E., and D. H. Arner. 1967. Winter food available to the wild turkey in a hardwood forest. *Proceedings of the Annual Conference of the Southeastern Association of Game and Fish Commissioners* 21:123–128.

Kiel, W. H., Jr. 1969. The ecology of the Rio Grande turkey in south Texas. In *Annual Report,* pp. 69–73, Caesar Kleberg Research in Wildlife Ecology, College of Agriculture, Texas A. & M. University, College Station, Tex., 270 pp.

Knoder, C. E. 1960. An aging technique for juvenile wild turkeys based on the rate of primary feather molt and growth. *Proceedings of the First National Wild Turkey Symposium* 1:159–176.

Knott, A. A. 1888. Turkeys in the nation. *Forest and Stream* 31:45–46.

Korschgen, L. J. 1967. Feeding habits and foods. In *The Wild Turkey and Its Management,* O. H. Hewitt, ed., pp. 137–198. The Wildlife Society, Washington, D.C.

————. 1970. Soil-food-chain-pesticide wildlife relationships in aldrin-treated fields. *Journal of Wildlife Management* 34(1):186–199.

————. 1972. Spring foods of wild turkeys in Missouri. *Proceedings of the Second National Wild Turkey Symposium,* Columbia, Mo. (at press).

Kozicky, E. L. 1948. Life history and management of the wild turkey *(Meleagris gallopavo silvestris)* in Pennsylvania. Ph.D. dissertation, Pennsylvania State College, University Park, Pa.

Lane, H. H. 1926. Oklahoma. In V. E. Shelford, *Naturalists' Guide to the Americas.* Baltimore: The Williams and Wilkins Company.

Latham, R. M. 1956. *Complete Book of the Wild Turkey.* Harrisburg, Pa.: Stackpole Company, 265 pp.

————. 1959. Some considerations concerning the emergency winter feeding of wild turkeys in northern states. *Transactions of the North American Wildlife and Natural Resources Conference* 24:414–421.

Lawson, J. 1937. *The History of North Carolina* (1714). Richmond, Va.

Leopold, Aldo. 1931. *Game Survey of the North Central States.* Madison, Wis.: Democrat Printing Co., 299 pp.

Leopold, A. S. 1944. The nature of heritable wildness in turkeys. *The Condor* 46:133–197.

————. 1953. Intestinal morphology of gallinaceous birds in relation to food habits. *Journal of Wildlife Management* 17(2):197–203.

Levon, Lee. 1959. The present status of the wild turkey in New Mexico. *Proceedings of the First National Wild Turkey Symposium* 1:37–42.

Lewis, J. B. 1966. Hybridization between wild and domestic turkeys in Missouri. *Journal of Wildlife Management* 30(3):431–432.

————. 1967. Management of the Eastern turkey in the Ozarks and Bottomland Hardwoods. In *The Wild Turkey and Its Management,* O. H. Hewitt, ed., pp. 371–408. The Wildlife Society, Washington, D.C., 589 pp.

Lewis, J. C. 1962. Wild turkeys in Allegan County, Michigan. Master of Science thesis, Michigan State University, East Lansing, Mich., 35 pp.

————. 1964. Populations of wild turkey in relation to fields. *Proceedings of the Annual Conference of the Southeastern Game and Fish Commissioners* 18:49–56.

————. 1967. Physical characteristics and physiology. In *The Wild Turkey and Its Management.* O. H. Hewitt, ed., pp. 45–72. The Wildlife Society, Washington, D.C.

Ligon, J. S. 1946. *History and Management of Merriam's Wild Turkey.* University of New Mexico Publication in Biology, Number 1, Albuquerque, N.M., 84 pp.

MacDonald, Duncan. 1961. Hunting season weights of New Mexico wild turkeys. *Journal of Wildlife Management* 25(4):442–444.

————. 1963. Trapping and marking Merriam's wild turkeys. *Proceedings of the Annual Conference of the Western Association of Game and Fish Commissioners* 43:196–201.

McDowell, R. D. 1956. *Productivity of the Wild Turkey in Virginia.* Commission of Game and Inland Fish, Technical Bulletin 1, Richmond, Va., 44 pp.

McIlhenny, E. A. 1914. *The Wild Turkey and Its Hunting.* New York: Doubleday-Page and Company, 245 pp.

Margolf, P. H., J. A. Harper, and E. W. Callenbach. 1947. *Response of Turkeys to Artificial Illumination.* Pennsylvania Agricultural Experiment Station Bulletin Number 486.

Marsden, S. J., and J. H. Martin. 1955. *Turkey Management.* 6th ed. Danville, Ill.: Interstate Press, 242 pp.

Martin, A. C., H. S. Zim, and A. L. Nelson. 1951. *American Wildlife and Plants.* New York: Dover Publications, Inc., 500 pp.

Meanley, B. 1956. Foods of the wild turkey in the White River bottomlands of southeastern Arkansas. *The Wilson Bulletin* 68(4):305–311.

Moore, R. T. 1938. A new race of wild turkey. *The Auk* 55:112–115.

Mosby, H. S. 1972. National status—the 30 year look. *Proceedings of the Second National Wild Turkey Symposium,* Columbia, Mo. (at press).

————, and C. O. Handley. 1943. *The Wild Turkey in Virginia: Its Status, Life History, and Management.* Virginia Commission of Game and Inland Fisheries, Richmond, Va., 281 pp.

Olsen, M. W., and S. J. Marsden. 1956. Parthenogenesis in eggs of

Bibliography

Beltsville Small White turkeys. *Poultry Science* 35:674–682.

Olsen, S. J. 1968. *Fish, Amphibians and Reptile Remains from Archaeological Sites*. I. Peabody Museum, Harvard University, Cambridge, Mass., 137 pp.

Parker, W. A., III. 1967. A quantitative study of available late winter foods of the Eastern wild turkey *Meleagris gallopavo silvestris* on the longleaf pine region of Mississippi. Master of Science thesis, Mississippi State University, State College, Miss., 24 pp.

Petersen, L. E., and A. H. Richardson. 1972. Merriam's wild turkey in the Black Hills of South Dakota. *Proceedings of the Second National Wild Turkey Symposium,* Columbia, Mo. (at press)

Poole, E. L. 1938. Weights and wing areas in North American birds. *The Auk* 55:511–517.

Portmann, A. 1961. Sensory organs: skins, taste, and olfaction. In *Biology and Comparative Physiology of Birds,* A. J. Marshall, pp. 37–48. New York. Academic Press, 168 pp.

Powell, J. A. 1963. Florida wild turkey movements and longevity as determined by band returns. *Proceedings of the Annual Conference of the Southeastern Association of Game and Fish Commissioners* 17:16–19.

————. 1965. *The Florida Wild Turkey.* Technical Bulletin 8, Florida Game and Fresh Water Fish Commission, Tallahassee, Fla., 28 pp.

Pumphrey, R. J. 1961. Sensory organs: vision; Sensory organs: hearing. In *Biology and Comparative Physiology of Birds.* A. J. Marshall, Part I, pp. 55–68; Part II, pp. 69–86. New York: Academic Press, 468 pp.

Raybourne, J. W. 1968. Telemetry of turkey movements. Master of Science thesis, Virginia Polytechnic Institute, Blacksburg, Va., 65 pp.

Reeves, R. H., and W. G. Swank. 1955. *Food Habits of Merriam's Turkey.* Arizona P-R Project W-49-R-3, 15 pp.

Ritchie, W. A. 1944. The pre-Iroquoian occupations of New York State. *Rochester Museum Arts and Science Memoirs* 1:1–416.

Rush, Gene. 1972. Some techniques in establishing and managing the Eastern wild turkey (*Meleagris gallopavo silvestris*). *Proceedings of the Second National Wild Turkey Symposium,* Columbia, Mo.

149

(at press).

Rutledge, A. H. 1924. *Days Off in Dixie*. Garden City, N.Y.: Doubleday, Page & Co., 298 pp.

Sadler, K. C. 1961. Grit selectivity by the female pheasant during egg production. *Journal of Wildlife Management* 25(3):339–341.

Santleben, A. 1910. *A Texas Pioneer*. Washington D.C., Neale Publishing Co., 321 pp.

Schleidt, M. 1955. Untersuchungen uber die Auslosung des Kollerns beim Truthahn (Meleagris gallopavo). *Z. Tierpsychologie* 11:417–435.

Schorger, A. W. 1957. The beard of the wild turkey. *The Auk* 74(3): 441–446.

———. 1960. The crushing of *Carya* nuts in the gizzard of the turkey. *The Auk* 77:337–340.

———. 1966. *The Wild Turkey: Its History and Domestication*. Norman, Okla.: University of Oklahoma Press, 625 pp.

———. 1970. A new subspecies of Meleagris gallopavo. *The Auk* 87(1):168–170.

Schwartzkopff, J. 1955. On the hearing of birds. *The Auk* 72(4):340–347.

Scott, H. M. 1933. The effect of age and holding temperatures on hatchability of turkey and chicken eggs. *Poultry Science* 12:49–54.

———, and L. F. Payne. 1934. The effect of gonadectomy on the secondary sexual characteristics of the bronze turkey (*M. gallopavo*). *Journal of Experimental Zoology* 69(1):123–131.

Smyth, J. F. D. 1784. *A Tour in the United States of America*. Vol. I. London: Collections of the American Antiquarian Society.

Speake, D. W., L. H. Barwick, H. O. Hillestad, and Walter Stickney. 1969. Some characteristics of an expanding turkey population. *Proceedings of the Annual Conference of the Southeastern Association of Game and Fish Commissioners* 23:46–58.

Stoddard, H. L., Sr. 1963. *Maintenance and Increase of the Eastern Wild Turkey on Private Lands on the Coastal Plain of the Deep Southeast*. Bulletin 3, Tall Timbers Research Station, Tallahassee, Fla., 49 pp.

Bibliography

Sturkie, P. D. 1965. *Avian Physiology*. Ithaca, N.Y.: Comstock Publishing Associates, 766 pp.

Suetsuga, H. Y., and K. E. Menzel. 1963. Wild turkey introductions in Nebraska. *Transactions of the North American Wildlife and Natural Resources Conference* 28:297–307.

Thomas, C. H. 1955. Relationships of wild turkey social and spatial behavior to management. Master of Science thesis, Oklahoma State University, Stillwater, Okla., 67 pp.

Thomas, J. W., C. V. Hoozer, and R. G. Marburger. 1964a. Notes and color aberrancies in the Rio Grande wild turkey. *The Wilson Bulletin* 76(4):381–382.

——, ——, and ——. 1964b. Wild turkey behavior affected by the presence of golden eagles. *The Wilson Bulletin* 76(4):384–385.

——, ——, and ——. 1966. Wintering concentrations and seasonal shifts in range in the Rio Grande wild turkey. *Journal of Wildlife Management* 30(1):34–49.

——, J. C. Pack, J. D. Gill, and R. W. Bailey. 1972a. Even-aged management, turkeys, and turkey hunters—a new study. *Proceedings of the Second National Wild Turkey Symposium*, Columbia, Mo. (at press).

——, R. G. Marburger, and C. V. Hoozer. 1972b. Rio Grande turkey migrations as related to harvest regulations in Texas. *Proceedings of the Second National Wild Turkey Symposium*, Columbia, Mo. (at press).

Twedt, C. M. 1961. Fall food habits of the Merriam's wild turkey in western South Dakota. Master of Science thesis, South Dakota State College of Agriculture and Mechanic Arts, Brookings, S.D., 50 pp.

Uhlig, H. S., and R. W. Bailey. 1952. Factors influencing the distribution and abundance of the wild turkey in West Virginia. *Journal of Wildlife Management* 16(1):24–32.

Walls, D. T. 1964. The wild turkey and ruffed grouse in Cameron County, Pennsylvania. Master of Science thesis, Pennsylvania State University, University Park, Pa., 104 pp.

Watts, C. R. 1968. Rio Grande turkeys in the mating season. *Trans-*

151

actions of the North American Wildlife and Natural Resources Conference 33:205–210.

———. 1972. Rio Grande turkeys in the mating season. *Proceedings of the Second National Wild Turkey Symposium,* Columbia, Mo. (at press).

——— and A. W. Stokes. 1971. The social order of turkeys. *Scientific American* 224(6):112–118.

Webb, L. G. 1941. Acorns, a favorite food of wild turkey in winter. *Alabama Conservationist* 13(4):5, 14, 15.

———. 1963. Utilization of domestic forage crops by deer and wild turkeys with notes on insects inhabiting the crop. *Proceedings of the Annual Conference of the Southeastern Association of Game and Fish Commissioners* 17:92–99.

Webb, W. S. 1946. Indian knoll site OH2, Ohio County, Kentucky. *Anthropological Archaeology Report* 3(1):111–340.

Welty, J. C. 1962. *The Life of Birds.* Philadelphia: W. B. Saunders Company, 546 pp.

Wetmore, Alexander. 1956. A check list of the fossil and prehistoric birds of North America and the West Indies. *Smithsonian Miscellaneous Collection* 131(5):1–105.

Wheeler, R. J. 1948. *The Wild Turkey in Alabama.* Alabama Conservation Department, 92 pp.

Williams, L. E., Jr. 1959. Analysis of wild turkey field sign: an approach to census. Master of Science thesis, Alabama Polytechnic Institute, Auburn, Ala., 74 pp.

———. 1964. A recurrent color aberrancy in the wild turkey. *Journal of Wildlife Management* 28(1):148–151.

———. 1966. Capturing wild turkeys with alpha-chloralose. *Journal of Wildlife Management* 30(1):50–56.

———. 1971. Tarso-metatarsus color in wild turkeys. *Journal of Wildlife Management* 35(3):550–553.

———, and D. H. Austin. 1969. Leg spurs on female wild turkeys. *The Auk* 86(3):561–562.

———, ———, N. F. Eichholz, T. E. Peoples, and R. W. Phillips. 1968. A study of nesting turkeys in southern Florida. *Proceedings of the Annual Conference of the Southeastern Game and Fish Commissioners* 22:16–29.

Bibliography

———, ———, T. E. Peoples, and R. W. Phillips. 1971. Laying data and nesting behavior of wild turkeys. *Proceedings of the Annual Conference of the Southeastern Association of Game and Fish Commissioners* 25:90–106.

———, ———, ———, and ———. 1972a. Observations on movement, development, and behavior of wild turkey broods. *Proceedings of the Second National Wild Turkey Symposium*, Columbia, Mo. (at press).

———, ———, ———, and ———. 1972b. Capturing turkeys with oral drugs. *Proceedings of the Second National Wild Turkey Symposium*, Columbia, Mo. (at press).

Wormington, H. M. 1959. *Prehistoric Indians of the Southwest.* Popular Series Number 7, The Denver Museum of Natural History, 191 pp.

Wright, A. H. 1914. Early records of the wild turkey. *The Auk* 31: 334–358, 463–473.

Wunz, G. A. 1971. Evaluation of game-farm and wild-trapped turkeys in Pennsylvania. *Pennsylvania Game News* 42(1):20–26, 43–44.

Zimmer, J. T. 1924. *The Wild Turkey.* Field Museum of Natural History, Zoological Leaflet 6, Chicago, Ill.

153

Index

Italic page numbers indicate illustrations